# on track ...

# Roxy Music

every album, every song

Michael Kulikowski

SONICBOND

sonicbondpublishing.com

Sonicbond Publishing Limited
www.sonicbondpublishing.co.uk
Email: info@sonicbondpublishing.co.uk

First Published in the United Kingdom 2024
First Published in the United States 2024

British Library Cataloguing in Publication Data:
A Catalogue record for this book is available from the British Library



ISBN 978-1-78952-335-5



Typeset in ITC Garamond Std & ITC Avant Garde Gothic
Printed and bound in England

Graphic design and typesetting: Full Moon Media

**Follow us on social media:**
Twitter: https://twitter.com/SonicbondP
Instagram: www.instagram.com/sonicbondpublishing_/
Facebook: www.facebook.com/SonicbondPublishing/

Linktree QR code:

*on track ...*

# Roxy Music

every album, every song

Michael Kulikowski

SONICBOND

sonicbondpublishing.com

**Dedication**

For Hubert

# Acknowledgements

In his secret life, Neil Tennant was a roundhead general. In mine, I write about popular music for a living. There was a time when I wanted to be a rock star (What child since the mid-1960s hasn't?), but my lack of discernable musical ability was a deterrent. Writing came more easily, and since adolescence, I have been making up record reviews in my head and obsessively rewriting them till I think they're right. While this does waste brain space that could go to something more obviously useful, I like to think that the mental discipline of writing imaginary reviews has made me better at my day job as an academic historian. Rock and pop entered my consciousness at age 12 or so, Roxy Music a couple of years later, and along with Bowie and Springsteen, Roxy have been the centre of my musical taste ever since.

For the past three-quarters of a century, give or take, pop music has been a vital component in adolescent identity formation. But for some people, its importance recedes as the 30th birthday approaches. That is one reason why record shops are so vitally important. In early life, they help young people find themselves, whether as an antidote to, or reinforcement of, the teenage proclivity to snobbery and tribalism. Later, after one has outgrown the need for constant in-group approval (no one stays cool past 40), record shops provide a rare space for a casual, transitory, but nevertheless meaningful community based on shared tastes. Along with Amoeba, Rough Trade, Newbury Comics, Sam the Record Man and HMV's Canadian flagship on Yonge Street in Toronto, the shops that have meant the most to me over the years have been Bleecker Bob's, Cheap Thrills, The Diskery, Jelly's, Kop's, Music in a Different Kitchen, the Princeton Record Exchange, Swordfish, Turn it Up, Vintage Vinyl (Fords) and Vortex, a handful of which survive to this day. In the present day, let me give a shout-out to Fez Records (Axemann, PA), Beautiful World Syndicate, Cratediggaz, Digital Underground, Molly's Books and Records and the eternal Repo (all Philadelphia), along with extra special props to Nick and Janis at Long in the Tooth in Philly, and Josh Ferko's Stax of Trax in State College. Finally, I try to avoid shopping for music online, which takes most of the fun out of it, but I make an exception for Luke Jackson of Luke's Records, whose one-man show is the best in the business.

Friends and family also merit recognition – Clay Webster, Josh Rosenblum, and the late Joe Miklojcik from formative days at school and university; a handful of historian colleagues with loosely overlapping tastes (Hugh Elton, Jared Farmer, Geoffrey Greatrex, Guy Halsall and Matthew Restall, despite Elton John); Nevaeh Paige and Connor and Ruby Henson-Stroud for letting me lecture them about music; and June Griffin, who was with me at the beginning for Roxy. When we broke up a great many years ago, she found herself with my copy of *Street Life: 20 Greatest Hits*, and I with hers of *Stranded*. Decades later, I remain aware of having had the better part of that deal. Latterly, I'm profoundly grateful to Ellen Stroud for coming with me to more Bryan Ferry concerts than any non-obsessive should have to see.

Most of all, though, there's my uncle Hubert Kulikowski, who bought me my first record, took me to my first concert, and generally helped a musically obsessed teenager navigate familial indifference and parental disapproval. We don't have many musical tastes in common, but I'm dedicating this book to him anyway, as long overdue thanks.

# *on track ...*

# Roxy Music

## Contents

# Introduction

Roxy Music have existed for just over 50 years. Their eponymous first album appeared in June 1972. Just shy of a decade later, in May 1982, they released *Avalon*, their eighth and final studio album.

Two moments – both fairly recent – capture the personal and musical dynamic that makes Roxy's work together so different from all its members' other projects, solo and collective. 29 March 2019: the Barclays Center in Brooklyn. Roxy Music were about to be inducted into the Rock 'n' Roll Hall of Fame, a full 21 years after they first became eligible for that dubious honour. There, buttonholed on the red carpet, were Phil Manzanera and Andy Mackay, two of the three constants in the Roxy story. Manzanera – 6'1" and relaxed in an impeccable blue suit and open-necked shirt – was all smiles, answering the usual vacuous questions with soft-spoken good humour. Mackay – also very tall but saying very little – looked like an eccentric provincial lecturer in an absurd plaid suit. Rather unexpectedly, Eddie Jobson was also there. Though his electric violin and keyboards had been all over the three albums he made with Roxy, he was long ago airbrushed out of the band's story. He had arrived at the Center first, though his garrulous Teesside chatter petered out once Manzanera and Mackay had arrived. There was as yet no sign of Bryan Ferry.

When it was time for the induction itself, Duran Duran's Simon Le Bon and Andy Taylor bounded on to the stage, mugging shamelessly for the cameras. They seemed to know that – despite their far greater wealth and fame – they will never approach the artistic achievement or cultural impact of the band they were there to honour. On they came – Ferry first, smiling, waving; Manzanera and Mackay trailing slightly to Ferry's right, then Jobson a little further back still. Three of them settled together close to the mic, with Ferry to the fore. Jobson took a place to Ferry's left, perhaps three feet away. As Ferry began to speak, Jobson stepped across behind him to say something to Manzanera, who smiled, laughing agreeably, and mouthed what was perhaps a reassurance. Jobson retreated out of the camera frame again, and, as ever, the spotlight stayed on Ferry. He has aged well, still exuding the rumpled elegance he perfected in his late forties. Naturally, he would be the one to deliver the group's acceptance speech. Having scrubbed all trace of County Durham from his accent in the 1970s, he was now letting himself sound Northern again. The long-standing trace of a labiodental 'r' in his pronunciation has become stronger with age: so 'price' sounds a bit like 'pwice'. He thanked the audience and fans around the world and then began thanking all the musicians who played with the band over the years, 'especially Paul Thompson and Brian Eno'. As Manzanera led the audience in thunderous applause, Ferry nodded along for a full five seconds and then gestured to his left: 'and Eddie Jobson, who, who's here, with, with us tonight. Great'. Then he made a joke ('Quite a long list, I'm afraid') about how many bass players he was going to have to thank.

The night's performance was alright. Manzanera and Mackay did their thing, and Jobson attacked the climactic violin solo on 'Out Of The Blue' like a vengeful demon. Perhaps deliberately, the band played only two tracks from the Jobson albums, one of which was 'Love Is The Drug', on which he barely featured. They were backed by Ferry's regular touring band led by guitarist Chris Spedding – an eternal sideman who can play anything and never threatens to upstage the boss – and by Jorja Chalmers, who combines runway model looks with multi-instrumental virtuosity. Since none of them were allowed the solo spots they get at Ferry's solo shows, they effaced themselves gracefully to make space for Phil and Andy. Ferry? He gave it the professional sheen he brings to even his most perfunctory live appearances, but it was clearly effortful, and he looked pained: not in control of the situation and not liking that fact. His solo shows are meticulously choreographed, whereas this hasty reunion was necessarily under-rehearsed. Ferry seemed like he wanted to be somewhere else.

Three years later, September 2022. The Philadelphia evening was warm and damp when Roxy brought their 50th-anniversary tour to the Mann Center – an outdoor amphitheatre that seats 4,500 in a covered pavilion and another 10,000 or so on the open lawn and terrace. The show was not sold out, even after it was moved there from the sports arena at which it had originally been scheduled. That was never realistic. At their very peak, Roxy never breached the US top 20. But the audience was excited, with virtually no one under 50 in the crowd: maybe a handful of 20-somethings humouring their parents. Most of us never expected to have this chance – I was only 11 when Roxy toured *Avalon*, and I couldn't afford to attend the 30th-anniversary tour. This meant that however many times I'd seen Ferry solo (a lot: I've lost count), I'd never seen Roxy and had more-or-less given up hope. I suspect that went for many of those there that night – it certainly did for the women to either side of me, determined not to let their indifferent male companions spoil their fun. The three of us were on our feet from the start.

Everyone was expecting a polished performance. The tour had gone like clockwork, the same 20-song set rolled out in a slightly different order at every show. St. Vincent opened and was everything a warm-up act should be, including efficient. The lights went down as the *Avalon* version of 'India' came over the sound system and the band filed onstage in semi-darkness. Along with Ferry, Mackay, Manzanera and original drummer Paul Thompson, ten other musicians were up there – two keyboard players, a percussionist, a second guitarist, three backup singers (including Fonzi Thornton, a stalwart of Roxy/Ferry albums and tours since *Avalon*), the equally reliable Neil Jason on bass, and Jorja Chalmers on keys and sax. Ferry was looking positively boyish as the electric piano chords of 'Re-Make/Re-Model' kicked in. He was smiling, Manzanera was smiling, and Thompson bashed the hell out of his kit as if he were still 25. Mackay was resplendent in a ludicrous tartan suit – the only member there to have carried the sartorial provocations of Roxy's early years into old age. Meanwhile, Chalmers was conducting the band at stage left, keyboardist and musical director Christian Gulino doing the same stage right, and both of them taking their cues from Manzanera. I had never seen this before – Ferry relinquishing his iron grip on the stage, allowing others to lead the band, and letting himself sing and play with (impeccably rehearsed) abandon.

The set offered no surprises and was firmly anchored on the group's first two and last two albums – there was nothing from *Stranded*, and only one song each from the following three albums (all obligatory: 'Out Of The Blue', 'Love Is The Drug' and 'Dance Away'). The sound was gorgeously engineered, and the lighting and backdrop sumptuous, in saturated but tasteful colours. The band were there to play music, not stage a spectacle. Deep cuts like 'The Bogus Man' got a rare airing in punchy and abbreviated arrangements. The *Avalon* tracks gained some heft and brawn from Thompson, and only 'Dance Away' (which Manzanera has claimed they all dread playing) seemed a bit perfunctory. Ferry's voice was – of course – a shadow of its former self, and some songs were transposed to a lower key to accommodate his reduced vocal range. Mackay seemed a little bit absent, and one sometimes wondered if Chalmers might not have been offering discreet, supportive doubling of his sax parts. But it didn't matter. Most of the audience had heard facsimiles of these songs on Ferry tours, yet this was very different. Manzanera, in particular, remains inimitable. His solos can be copied but not reproduced, and when he let loose on 'Out Of The Blue' and 'In Every Dreamhome A Heartache', it was clear that Roxy Music really do play their songs better than anyone else. Ferry must know that too, and it showed, especially in the final dash through 'Love Is The Drug', 'Editions Of You' and 'Do The Strand'. As the last chords of 'Jealous Guy' faded and the cheers erupted, Ferry summoned Thompson out from behind his riser, and the four original band members linked hands and took a bow, all smiling as if genuinely pleased to be there. I'd like to think they were. That tour was almost certainly the end of the Roxy Music story. If so, it's a happy ending. Finally, after 50 years of Roxy, Bryan Ferry seems to have managed to relax.

## Beginnings

Roxy's origin story has been told many times. It starts with Bryan Ferry moving to London in 1968 when he was 23. He was born in Washington, Co. Durham, in 1945. His father – a prize-winning ploughman in his youth – had taken a job looking after pit ponies when the Great Depression struck. Bryan's mother had worked in a factory during the decade Fred Ferry courted her. Their family was very poor but looked on education as a way out of the working class. There was never any real chance of Ferry going down the pits or into the Tyne and Wear shipyards. He passed the 11-plus exam, winning a place at Washington Grammar Technical School in 1957, and eventually found himself studying fine art at Newcastle University, the youngest of the redbrick universities. Beginning his course in 1964, Ferry remained at Newcastle till 1968, studying for one year under the famous pop artist Richard Hamilton. He sang in various local bands, most notably the Gas Board, with fellow students Graham Simpson and John Porter, trying to sound American and performing mostly soul standards. Ferry and Simpson – who was a couple of years older than Ferry – aspired to more than playing bingo halls and workingmen's clubs, which, for provincial youngsters before and since, meant moving to the capital. There, Ferry worked as a van driver and then a ceramic arts teacher at the Mary Boon School for girls in Hammersmith. He was sacked for spending more time playing records and letting the schoolgirls gossip and complain to him about their boyfriends than he did teaching ceramics.

By then, his musical ambitions were beginning to bear some fruit. At Simpson's urging, Ferry had advertised for a band, starting with a keyboard player. That brought him into contact with Andy Mackay – not a keyboard player, but proficient on saxophone and oboe. Mackay grew up a working-class Londoner who, like Ferry, had benefitted from post-war reforms in education. He attended grammar school and became a chorister of Saint Margaret's, Westminster, before studying English and music at Reading. There, he met a postman's son from East Anglia – the resplendently named Brian Peter George St. Baptiste de la Salle Eno, who'd landed at Winchester School of Art after running through his grant money at Ipswich and abandoning his program there. Now absorbed into the universities of Southampton and Suffolk, respectively, Winchester and Ipswich were – with the era's other art colleges – a vital outlet in which bright working-class youngsters could do something besides learn how to labour. Or, as Mackay would acidly put it in a 1975 interview with the journalist Chris Salewicz: 'That's the trouble with free education – you get all these working-class boys educated beyond their station'. What Richard Hamilton had been for Ferry, Roy Ascott was for Eno, and both he and Mackay also played with London-based avant-garde composer Cornelius Cardew.

With Eno and Mackay joining Ferry and Simpson in early 1971, they fiddled around for several months, seeing what they could do by way of Ferry's songwriting, Mackay's oboe (outlandish in a rock context), and Eno's determined deconstruction of whatever conventional music forms emerged. They tried out a drummer or two until Ferry turned to Paul Thompson, a fellow Geordie, five years younger than the rest of them. Unlike them, he had left school at 16 and hadn't pursued further education, which for many years would give him an undeserved reputation with journalists as a primitive brickie adopted by a tribe of clever musos. In reality, he'd served real time on the Northern club circuit and had even backed Billy Fury in the studio, which meant he had more practical musical experience than the rest of the band combined. A number of guitarists were also tested out, including Roger Bunn, who played on the demo tape Ferry spent much of 1971 touting to record companies and music journalists. Philip Targett Adams – guitarist from the recently disbanded Quiet Sun – also auditioned for the as-yet-unnamed band. Even younger than Thompson, Adams went by his South American mother's surname of Manzanera, which allowed him to disguise his birth into the British establishment – his father had worked for the British Overseas Airways Corporation, and Phil had himself been a boarder at Dulwich College. Ferry turned Manzanera down, but he stayed in the band's orbit for the next few months. Though his audition had been unimpeachable, Ferry had his eyes on name player David O'List – an accomplished and flashy performer who'd briefly been a 1960s superstar with The Nice but was now at a loose end after Keith Emerson split the band and formed Emerson, Lake & Palmer.

With O'List inducted into the fledgling band in October 1971, their lineup seemed set, even as most of the group were still working day jobs – Thompson on a building site, Mackay teaching music at Holland Park Comprehensive, Manzanera at a travel agency, and Ferry as a supply teacher two days a week. He continued trying to sell the demos to various record companies but with a conspicuous lack of success. Not only were the demos terribly amateurish, they were terribly weird. Also, the band had no following and hadn't paid its dues on the live circuit the way an up-and-coming unit should. Ferry – who'd had his fill of grinding out covers in workingmen's clubs with the Gas Board – had no intention of subjecting Roxy to that kind of hard graft. Instead, he used his contacts in the art world to get gigs at private parties, and even at the Tate Museum, before audiences of rich dilettantes. That was sufficient to get a bit of a buzz going. But it was a 12 December 1971 *Melody Maker* piece by Richard Williams (who liked their demo) that gave the band the opportunity to break through. 'Although it was recorded on a small home tape machine in what sounds like a Dutch barn', Williams wrote, 'it carries enough innovatory excitement to suggest that Roxy may well be head of the field in the avant-garde stakes'. Those stakes were raised a few days later when John Peel invited the band to perform on his *Sound Of The Seventies* show. Taped in just two hours on 4 January 1972, the tracks were broadcast on 21 January and 18 February. Though rudimentary, all five songs ('If There Is Something', 'The Bob (Medley)', 'Would You Believe?', 'Sea Breezes' and 'Re-Make/Re-Model') were already recognizable as the numbers that would be recorded more competently for *Roxy Music*. (Bootlegged countless times, Roxy's three Peel sessions and one *BBC In Concert* of 1972 were released legitimately on the 2018 deluxe edition of the first album.)

Finding the band championed by both *Melody Maker* magazine and the taste-making Peel, Ferry decided to aim high and tried to secure a deal with E.G. Management, who had luminaries like King Crimson, Emerson, Lake & Palmer and Marc Bolan in their portfolio. Ferry was deeply impressed with the effortless public school charm of the firm's co-founder, David Enthoven. (His partner John Gaydon had just bowed out to go into film production.) Enthoven wanted to sign a solo Ferry, not this weird band – a suggestion the singer curtly dismissed. Still, Enthoven was intrigued enough to audition the band live in an abandoned movie palace in Wandsworth and liked what he saw. The deal was signed on 14 February 1972 and, in celebration, Mackay quit his teaching job at half-term. Enthoven agreed to put up £5,000 to record the first record, which E.G. would then flog to a suitable label. But before that, O'List was asked to leave the band. His status in the music business meant he never felt obliged to join the others in humping equipment in and out of shows, and he'd proven himself to be reluctant to conform too closely to Ferry's vision of the music. Ferry called Manzanera, ostensibly to offer him a gig as a sound mixer, and then put him through another audition when he turned up. As Manzanera told Paul Sinclair of *Super Deluxe Edition* in 2018, he'd 'learnt the stuff beforehand. I didn't tell them'. And so, Manzanera got the job, disappointing his mother, who'd expected him to go to university. With the new lineup complete, February 1972 marked the end of the beginning of the Roxy Music story. Next came *Roxy Music,* the album, and their peerless first single 'Virginia Plain'.

## Roxy Music (1972)

Personnel:
Bryan Ferry: voice, piano
Graham Simpson: bass
Andrew Mackay: oboe, saxophone
Eno: synthesizer, tapes
Paul Thompson: drums
Phil Manzanera: guitar
Produced by Peter Sinfield
UK release date: June 1972
US release date: November 1972
Charts: UK: 10, USA: 193
Running time: 42:15

In June of 1972 – in one of those historical coincidences that only become significant in hindsight – RCA Victor released David Bowie's *The Rise And Fall Of Ziggy Stardust And The Spiders From Mars*, and Island put out *Roxy Music*. Glam rock was born that day and so too was one of the great inspirations for punk, post-punk, futurism and the new romantics – a look and a sound, calculated – as Dick Hebdige put it in his seminal 1979 study *Subculture* – to 'challenge the notoriously pedestrian stereotypes available to working-class men and women'. Half a century on, *Ziggy* sounds like the fabulous rock 'n' roll record it was, and *Roxy Music* sounds like… nothing before or since. It is among the most *outré* rock LPs ever recorded. The mix is thin and reedy, the arrangements unexpected and frequently bizarre. The rhythm section is rock solid, but the sound has little bottom end. The other players, though obviously musically gifted, sound entirely untutored, the singing all over the place. Plus, self-proclaimed non-musician Eno kept injecting chaos into the already unruly context. Yet contemporary reviews were positive, and the non-album single 'Virginia Plain' drove the album to a very respectable number ten in the charts. But while it's easy to see how Bowie's canny image-making supercharged the impact of his relatively accessible music among the wider public, the sheer strangeness of *Roxy Music* (especially side two) must have been a challenge for the casual listener.

And before you even get to the music, there's the cover. Where does one start? A glossy gatefold with Kari-Ann Moller posed like a 1950s pinup, in pink and white taffeta negligée and satin-trimmed stole. Her makeup is garish, exaggerated almost to the point of ugliness. Her smile, if you can call it that, is more of a grimace, draining her alluring pose of all eroticism. But the visual allusion to the world of drive-ins, Varga girls and huge American cars is unmistakable while also quite different from the nostalgia peddled in *American Graffiti*, Showaddywaddy or *Happy Days*. It's a wholly home-grown vision that Ferry (credited with 'cover concept' on the gatefold) and his indispensable co-conspirators – art director Nick de Ville and designer Anthony Price ('clothes, make-up and hair') – actualised here.

Open the gatefold sleeve, and the image-making is even more in your face. Who are these people? Or actually, what are they? Each portrait is framed in the serrated edges of a vintage postcard – Phil Manzanera wearing oversized glasses like a fly's eyes, so absurd that Zoo-TV era Bono would have hesitated before wearing them; Mackay, facing Manzanera, back-combed rooster quiff, sax in one hand, chin and rouged cheek resting on the other hand. Beneath and between them is a three-quarter portrait of a balding androgyne in a leopard-print jacket and blue leopard-print shirt for contrast. On the other side of the gatefold, there's Ferry, even more spectacularly bequiffed than Mackay, in a tight black t-shirt and tiger-print blazer, lapels the size of propeller blades, with the trashy gold necklace of a greaser or a rent boy. Graham Simpson – the first of Roxy's countless bass players – is clearly the odd man out, in an embroidered collegiate jumper, his shirt's enormous surgeon cuffs turned back halfway up the arm. Finally, there's young Paul Thompson, looking straight at the camera, in a black jumpsuit and what might be a cuddly toy tiger stapled to his shoulder. Then throw in the PR-flak verbiage from 'Dr.' Simon Puxley (an actual English lit PhD) way ahead of its time as a parody of hollow art criticism and the capital-T Theory that would eat academic music criticism alive in the 1980s. (As an example, consult *Rock: The Primary Text* by Allan F. Moore, whose astute analysis of Roxy's first album is fatally undermined by the abstruse prose).

The cover of *Roxy Music* ought to have been much too much. But what saves it all is the way a clearly articulated post-modernist Pop Art agenda is undercut by amateurish execution. The vision is fully formed, but its reach far exceeds its grasp. From this baseline, the progress Ferry and the band were to make in less than a year was nothing short of miraculous. Roxy Mk I's *For Your Pleasure*, Mk II's *Stranded* and Eno's *Here Come The Warm Jets* were each markedly different, but each was the work of men who'd learned very quickly how to do what they had always intended to do. That's true of the artwork and the visual and verbal rhetoric, but most of all, it's true of the music.

Given how iconic *Roxy Music* has become, it's now hard to believe that it was recorded by an unsigned band who'd paid no dues on the live circuit and had worked up their entire repertoire in studio rehearsals – and the entire repertoire wound up on the LP because it was all the material they had. (That, by the by, was the first sign of Roxy's extraordinarily parsimonious writing process. Unlike the acres of outtakes and alternative versions from, say, The Rolling Stones, Roxy left behind almost nothing to interest the bootleggers.) The band's management, E.G., put up the funds (a mere £5,000: less than a tenth of what the Stones spent to make *Sticky Fingers*) to record the LP at Command Studios in Piccadilly, with ex-King Crimson lyricist Pete Sinfield producing. E.G. then licensed the album to Island Records when proprietor Chris Blackwell decided to take a punt on it despite not particularly caring for the music himself – the proposed sleeve art is said to have convinced him. Island put the album out without further input, and the mere fact of its being on Island – then a terribly hip label – made people look up and listen. A more interventionist producer and a big-name studio would no doubt have made for a better-sounding album, but also a more conventional one. What makes *Roxy Music* hold up so well after half a century is how unlike anything else it still sounds.

**'Re-Make/Re-Model'** (Ferry)
Cocktail party chatter fades in, with a hard cut to a slightly syncopated two-chord piano part, and suddenly, all hell breaks loose. Drums, sax, guitar, keyboards and whooshing noise from Eno hit you all at once, a shocking but also joyous aural assault. 'I tried, but I could not find a way': Ferry's voice is ragged, his pitch wobbles, and he's testing the limits of his vocal range, but it doesn't matter amid the sonic barrage. A man closer to 30 than 20, he nails the optimism, aspiration, and also the gnawing restlessness of early youth: 'Next time is the best time/We all know'. Every adolescent has surely felt that itch for the new. And then there's the backing vocal: Eno and Mackay chanting 'CPL 593H'. A number plate? Yes. And not just any number plate, but supposedly that of a beautiful woman Ferry glimpsed in passing *en route* to a festival. I say supposedly because it's the kind of story that sounds made up. If it had come from a Bowie or a Lou Reed, it almost certainly *would* be made up. With Ferry, one doesn't know. He's such an aesthete and such a connoisseur of the surface of things that the story might just be true.

The song's structure is fairly conventional: verse/instrumental/verse/instrumental. And apart from the number plate, the words are pretty conventional, too. Without a doubt, the best bit is the long instrumental outro, with the whole band chugging along before all the instruments but one drop out and somebody takes a two-bar solo mimicking an iconic tune from the past – Wagner's 'Ride Of The Valkyries', The Beatles' 'Day Tripper', Duane Eddy's 'Peter Gunn' and so on. Once they've each had their say, the music rumbles on, more and more slowly like a tape getting eaten by its player, until Eno ends things with a great splatter of electronic noise from his VCS3 synth. It's the first example of Roxy's enduring talent for great album openers (of their eight studio albums, only *Flesh + Blood* has a less-than-stellar first track) and a declaration of the band's having arrived. And the crowning glory? 'Re-Make/Re-Model' is not even the best track on the album.

**'Ladytron'** (Ferry)
*This* is the best track on the album. Its title is evocative but quite possibly meaningless, and as with the majority of Roxy's songs prior to *Siren* (1975), you won't find the title anywhere in the lyric. (That pattern, like much of the early Roxy aesthetic, surely takes its inspiration from the visual arts that were Ferry's first love: artists like Robert Rauschenberg, Eduardo Paolozzi, and

Ferry's teacher Richard Hamilton often gave their works enigmatic titles with no obvious connection to their content.) And, like the title, the sickly oboe part with which Mackay opens the track gives no hint of what lies ahead. 'You got me girl on the run around, run around/You've got me all around town'. It's the first hint of Ferry's later singing voice. Mellotron violins swan in behind him: 'Lady, if you want to find a lover/Then look no further'. Touching sincerity, or the first glimpse of the future lounge lizard: it's impossible to tell. Then you realize it's worse:

I'll move up close to you
I'll use you
And I'll confuse you
And then I'll lose you
Still you won't suspect me

It's actually the first appearance of the bogus man. Ferry's default persona is the hopeless romantic, but he's canny enough to recognize that the dark flipside of the hopeless romantic is the obsessive stalker. He would explore both sides of that line not just on the following year's *For Your Pleasure*, but also half a decade later on 'Still Falls The Rain'. Unlike the latter, 'Ladytron' is verbally concise and leaves plenty of space for the music to do the talking. It is perhaps the most musically inventive track on the whole album, with a pastoral opening that then changes to a loping swing for the first proper verse, a middle-eight in which Mackay goes berserk – his solo made stranger by Eno's treatment – and the harsher edge they all bring to the threatening last verse. Then, it closes with a coruscating Manzanera solo and three minutes of rapidly accelerating electronic noise as everyone races towards the phased climax. In and out of the setlist over the years, more recent iterations of 'Ladytron' have harnessed its wildness into something more songlike and predictable. This original is simply unhinged.

**'If There Is Something'** (Ferry)

This is the first of several *Roxy Music* tracks constructed in three parts. 'If There Is Something' stands out among them because each part is substantially different. Following the highwire act of 'Ladytron', this album rendition might seem to fly under the radar. But once you've heard the ten-minute workout it gets on *Viva!* (1976) (recorded in Newcastle in 1974), you realize what a fantastic composition it is, even in this embryonic version.

Country and western-style guitar walks us into a swinging Ferry vocal delivered in a deliberately unconvincing American accent. 'If there is something/That I might find' places us back in the youthful 'next time is the best time' of 'Re-make/Re-model'. Manzanera gets to give his technique a workout before Thompson's drum fill ushers in Eno's Moog wash and a heavily treated Mackay. Bryan's hopelessly in love now:

I would do anything for you
I would climb mountains
I would swim on the oceans blue

I would walk a thousand miles
Reveal my secrets
More than enough for me to share

But it's Ferry, and he can't help but cut apparent sincerity down to size:

I would put roses round our door
Sit in the garden
Growing potatoes by the score

Potatoes. There is nothing in the world less romantic than a potato, yet he makes it sound like the most precious gift he could possibly give. As he holds the final note of the verse with the help of his vibrato, a long instrumental passage begins. Eno gives Mackay's oboe an eerie, otherworldly keen, while Ferry's electric piano and a discreet Thompson drum part keep the rhythm going and hold everything together.

Finally, the vibe quietens, the piano becomes more emphatic, and Thompson's kick drum signals the start of something new as all the other instrumentation stops. 'Shake your head, girl, with your ponytail/Takes me right back (when you were young)'. This is Ferry at the top of his range, his voice cracking a little before breaking into an over-the-top chorus: 'Lift up your feet and put them on the ground/You used to walk upon (when you were young)' – when the hills were higher, the trees taller and the grass greener. It's ridiculous, ecstatic, celebratory, and while explicitly backwards-looking, it's not in the least bit nostalgic. That's where the song's power lies, and it became even more powerful once Ferry had a voice that could do justice to its grandeur.

**'2 H.B.'** (Ferry)

Ferry is obsessed with classic cinema. So too, though less obviously, is Phil Manzanera, who is on record about him and Ferry bonding over discussions of Humphrey Bogart. Bogart – to H.B. – is the oblique subject of this song. Or rather, not Bogart *per se*, but Bogart's Rick Blaine in *Casablanca*, which is not quite the same thing. By *Roxy Music* standards, '2 H.B.' has a fairly conventional structure. The sound fades up into an instrumental overture seemingly already in progress, but thereafter, it's verse/chorus/bridge/verse/chorus and a similarly languid fadeout. But within that, there's scope for one of the album's prettiest melodies, and also plenty of Eno noise bubbling along underneath. The lyrics are a window into Ferry's worldview – one that he seems to recognize in *Casablanca* and that we now know from his lifetime of songwriting. Ferry can be surprisingly aware of – and sensitive to – women's pain ('Here's looking at you kid/Wipe away tears'). He's also honest about the male capacity for casual emotional cruelty without celebrating it ('Hard to forget/At least not yet'). But at the same time, his genuine empathy recognises no space for female agency. The empathy is, in fact, predicated on the assumption that there's no such thing: 'You gave her away to the hero', he sings to Bogart's Rick. Just how much agency Ingrid Bergman's Ilsa has in getting on the plane to Portugal with Paul Henreid's Laszlo is a legitimate subject of debate. Ferry is in no doubt at all.

Were this only about the plot of a single classic movie, that would be one thing. But it's a consistent motif in the Ferry *oeuvre*. So too is 'Finding, not keeping's the lesson'. It requires a certain level of familiarity with *Casablanca* to grasp just how artful Ferry has been in constructing his lyrics. Bogart delivers the 'Here's looking at you, kid' line four times in the movie. In '2 H.B.', it's stated twice in each chorus. The song that immortalizes Rick and Ilsa's lost life in Paris is Herman Hupfeld's 'As Time Goes By', which the film turned into a standard. When Ferry got around to a throwaway album of jazz standards (as it was always inevitable that he would), he called the album *As Time Goes By* (1999) and opened with a version of that song. But it's not just about the doomed romance and the 'White jacket, hmm, black-tie wings too'. *Casablanca* is candid about the hard choices – moral, ethical, sexual and political – that war forces on people. It's a theme that Ferry cared enough about to return to on 'The Bob (Medley)'. And lest the analysis get too serious, remember that 2HB is also a pencil. Our Bryan; he just couldn't help it.

### **'The Bob (Medley)'** (Ferry)

By no means the album's best track, 'The Bob (Medley)' *is* probably its most interesting. 'Bob' is B.O.B.: the Battle of Britain – Britain's finest hour, fought three years before Ferry was born. Like every child of his generation, Ferry grew up with the aftermath and the collective memory of the war a constant presence. Britain had won the war but not the peace. Ferry was nine before rationing finally ended. Even worse, the post-war boom years had delivered prosperity very unequally, not least in the Co. Durham of his working-class childhood, where the pits or the docks lay at the end of the teenage dream. Ferry's dream was lived vicariously through the movies and the impossibly glamorous and affluent America they revealed. But what could any of that mean for the men and women who had come through the Depression only to fight the war? What could you say to people who'd been through hell and survived? You certainly couldn't expect them to understand you.

As the oldest members of the band, Ferry and Mackay would have been looking forward to 18 months of National Service after leaving school when it was abolished in 1960. Instead of the Malayan or Cyprus emergencies, they got art college and The Beatles, creating a generational chasm between them and men just a couple of years older. The rest of the band – younger and more definitively post-war – could enjoy a less ambivalent relationship to the culture (musical and otherwise) of their parents, grandparents and older siblings. 'The Bob' seems like Ferry's concerted attempt to imagine his way into the minds of his parents' generation – those who'd grown up in the shadow of the first war and faced adulthood in the reality of the second one. It's the same sort of task that Pete Townshend and Roger Waters repeatedly set for themselves, but Ferry does it with a refreshing lack of literalism.

'The Bob' is a song of three parts, opening with disconcerting Eno tape drones and a two-note piano figure buried in the mix. Then Thompson's drums cascade in, and Ferry raggedly shouts, 'I dreamed last night about your face', the face of someone 'So pure/Not for this world', over a menacing guitar riff. As the verse ends, quiet descends, and Mackay's oboe picks out a hushed melody while Eno lays down a sound collage of propellers, anti-aircraft guns and bombs. Then a piano starts to groove, and the track explodes into a jaunty major-key dance as a massed chorus of Ferrys sings 'Too many times beautiful/Too many times sad/Too many times wonderful/Too bad', with an air-raid siren just audible in the depths of the mix. Manzanera unleashes a rollicking guitar solo, sax and piano start to vibe, the guitar and sax fade out, and a piano leads us into a voiceover meant to sound like classic film dialogue ('But when the party was over and all was quiet and still, we walked together in the moonlight...'). Then, as at the start, Thompson's drums crash back in, and a tortured Ferry wails:

So in my dream you still loved me
Gave time reason, last night
But this was only life's story
Made simple, that's right

The menace lurking underneath is, this time, provided by Mackay's sax. Finally, the band exhausted, Eno delivers a wash of ambient hum as a crystalline piano part gives way to a symphonic finale of reverberating drums.

So much – too much – is going on here, but there's an outline of a story – a soldier off to war, a passionate parting, a memory lost in a dream even before the bombs started falling on the slums of London and the shipyards of Newcastle and Liverpool. Then leave, a dance and a party, and a blessed moment of release in the knowledge that you might all be dead tomorrow; a pause, a reverie, the forlorn hope that love will win in the end. Finally – reality obtruding, love forever lost, but a glimpse of life perfected while it lasted. Two lovers' lives, two sundered stories, the small, fractured loves of individuals given the grandeur of tragedy. All of that is in there – Ferry at his most oblique, because actually he's at his most personal. The closest analogue to it isn't musical; it's the three-volume war sequence in the twelve novels that make up Anthony Powell's *A Dance To The Music Of Time* (1951-1975).

For all that, 'The Bob' is a laboured track. It takes too much work to understand it, and some might wonder if it's even worth bothering to try. That you can still hear some of the nasal Geordie vowels Ferry was working hard to lose on this recording probably didn't help his affection for it. It's no surprise that the band pulled it from their repertoire as soon as they had enough material to do without it. But the track has gained stature with time, and its complexity seems earned. A mixed success is, by definition, partly successful. So is 'The Bob'.

**'Chance Meeting'** (Ferry)
This is perhaps the slightest track on the album without the haphazard creativity of the preceding or following numbers. The melody is very simple and made queasily portentous by being slowed to a crawl. There are no drums, the piano carrying the entire rhythm. Any hint of beauty is undermined by Manzanera's lashing at the guitar chords so loudly that he couldn't hear the rest of the track when he played them and by the heavily treated blasts of Mackay's sax. The song was seemingly inspired by David Lean's heartbreaking *Brief Encounter* (1945), set between the wars and one of the most perfect films ever made. Ferry's hopeless lyric is saturated in present *ennui* and past grief:

It seems like yesterday
When I first saw you
In your red dress, mine

There's also none of the self-aware irony he was to perfect over the next two years of composition. But Ferry rated this track highly since – as with the rather better '2 H.B.' – he re-recorded it as a solo B-side and later included that version on *Let's Stick Together* (1976). Manzanera, Mackay and Thompson must've liked it too since it was one of just eight tracks they could all agree to include in *Viva!,* the live album they put out after going on hiatus in 1976.

**'Would You Believe?'** (Ferry)
A divisive track. Some find it to be a brilliant forerunner to 'Do The Strand' on *For Your Pleasure*. Others hear only a pastiche or a parody of a 1950s rocker. Let's go with a brilliant pastiche. Saxophone intro and hesitant, questioning opening verse:

Would you believe
In all I do?
When the things
That I make
Are all for you

Then things speed up with piano vamps, Manzanera chops out some chords very similar to those on 'Re-Make/Re-Model', Mackay blasts out a one-note sax line and everyone starts hammering away all at once. 'Well I'm sure I'll love you all my life/And in the morning too'. It's another variation on that eternal Ferry conundrum: is it a one-night stand, or is it the real thing? The vocals on the chorus are a well-intentioned send-up of doo-wop, Ferry providing a counterpoint to Mackay and Eno's parts. Then, everyone takes a solo before the opening verse repeats. It's all good fun, but as with the rest of the album's less persuasive tracks, the letdown is Ferry's lead vocal, which is trying to do more than his voice is capable of. His pitch wobbles fatally in the intro, and the falsetto on the chorus is way beyond his range. Elsewhere on *Roxy Music*, he's teaching himself to use vibrato to hold notes and stay on key between them, but the tempo here is too fast for that, and everything gets away from him. Verdict? Technically, it's not terribly good, but is indisputably rather charming.

**'Sea Breezes'** (Ferry)
This is the longest track on the album, but, alas, it's not good enough to warrant its length. Again, it's a song in three parts. Here, two very similar soft and slow segments frame a slightly faster herky-jerky middle that never quite reaches liftoff. We start with a hushed woodwind and a lugubrious Ferry and then proceed through a wash of Eno treatments till the tempo changes and the drums kick in under a highly mobile bass line (Simpson's most estimable contribution to the album) that Andy Hendriksen placed very high in the mix. But the proggy white noise and instrumental dissonance are simply not as interesting as the same basic formula was on the 'The Bob (Medley)'. Mackay is less inventive, and Eno's treatments are too basic and hushed, almost stifled. Manzanera's solo makes little impression, and the lyric is slightly sub-par too: 'Even angels there make the same mistakes in love'? 'It's a shame to think about yesterday/It's a shame'? 'Alone, what a word, lonely'? It's what you'd get if you asked a computer to generate a Bryan Ferry lyric. The song is a disappointment, but one that stuck around for quite a while, turning up in setlists as late as 1976 (best heard on the often-bootlegged Stockholm Konserthus gig from that January), perhaps because it was more amenable to Ferry's improving voice and pitch control than were some of the album's wilder tracks. Of the four *Roxy Music* tracks Ferry remade as solo B-sides between 1973 and 1976, 'Sea Breezes' is the only one he didn't thoroughly rework in the process. Maybe he liked it too much, or maybe he couldn't think of anything to change, for better or worse.

**'Bitters End'** (Ferry)
Nothing about the whole second side of *Roxy Music* prepares you for the weirdest track they ever recorded. Note that title. It's not the bitter end, it's not the end of someone called Bitter, it's the ending of the bitters.

With another band, it might only have signalled an insecure command of punctuation. Not this one: Ferry and Mackay were teachers, and Phil was a public school boy. They knew their apostrophes. When the bitters end, so do the cocktails. The party's over. Cue more noise of background chatter, but now with added doo-wop backing, as, in just over two minutes, Roxy deliver the most unlikely of manifestos. They know they're going to eclipse their forebears and re-make/re-model popular music. We now know that the first line was 'At last the crimson chord cascades', but there was no lyric sheet with the album prior to the 2022 reissue, and it sounds like Ferry is singing 'crimson court', which could be heard as a challenge to King Crimson, for whom Roxy producer Sinfield had provided lyrics.

In the soaring mid-section (one can't call it a chorus), Ferry manages, if briefly, to command the croon he was to perfect in time for the following year's *For Your Pleasure*. As Ferry does his lost-lover schtick ('But now I know you've found another/So will someone please find me'), a choir of Enos and Mackays lay down a background chant of 'bizarre'. Yes, yes, you think, this *is* bizarre. And then the doo-wop backing returns, and so does Ferry:

Give now the host his claret cup
And watch Madeira's farewell drop
Note his reaction, acid sharp
Should make the cognoscenti think

It's as supremely arrogant an *au revoir* as 'Re-Make/Re-Model' was an introduction. But make the cognoscenti think it certainly did.

### 'Virginia Plain' b/w 'The Numberer' (single)

Personnel:
Bryan Ferry: voice, piano
Rik Kenton: bass
Andrew Mackay: oboe, saxophone
Eno: synthesizer, tapes
Paul Thompson: drums
Phil Manzanera: guitar
Produced by Peter Sinfield
UK release date: August 1972
US release date: October 1972
Charts: UK: 4, USA: -
Running time: 2:58/3:37

Roxy only released three stand-alone singles in their ten years together, and this was the first and best of them. The positive response to *Roxy Music* was something of a slow burn, and there were certainly no obvious surefire singles that could have been drawn from it. The band wanted a hit – none of them made a secret of their ambitions. That was an interesting, perhaps even bold, choice for 1972, when the gap that had opened between singles and album artists over the last four years of the 1960s had widened into a canyon. Serious rock fans were immensely snobbish towards singles that got everything they wanted to say across in three minutes at 45 RPM. (This is hard to believe in today's eclectic, on-demand musical landscape, but for confirmation, check out Philip Cato's *Crash Course For The Ravers* – a charming memoir of a West Midlands adolescence in the glam era.) Roxy were just about the only group confident or arrogant enough to aspire to both hit singles and hit albums. Also, a hit single would validate all the press attention the young band had thus far garnered: Eno, in particular, was starting to demonstrate an almost Bowie-level capacity for attention-grabbing quotes to match his completely over-the-top outfits. Mackay was reliably waspish about the music business and Roxy's contemporaries. Ferry – despite his self-belief and the grandiosity of his plans – was already a highly tentative interviewee, though he had not yet developed the pathological reticence he would display later in the decade. Manzanera – perhaps because of his relative youth – tended to be modestly self-deprecating with journalists. But not everyone in the band could handle the stress of their sudden notoriety. Always depressive, Graham Simpson spiralled into weeping incoherence. Ferry – with the ruthlessness that lurked beneath his soft-spoken exterior – sacked his old friend over the telephone after what Mackay recalled as 'a lot of soul searching and regret'.

As everyone moved on to promoting the album, and Ferry set himself to writing a hit, Roxy replaced Simpson with Rik Kenton on the recommendation of Pete Sinfield. Though Kenton lasted for no more than six months in the band, he not only played the bass line of one of the most iconic 1970s singles, but he also got to perform with the band on their first *Top Of The Pops* appearance. That was a spectacularly ramshackle affair. (Widely available online, it appears in relatively high resolution on the 2018 deluxe edition of *Roxy Music*.) Eno is off-camera almost the whole time, and it's Kenton – not Manzanera – who gets the fretboard closeups. And though it all looks like a bit of a disaster now, at the time, it propelled the single further up the charts to its eventual number four and pulled the album up in its wake to a healthy number ten. Not altogether surprisingly, an America in thrall to Lobo, the Guess Who and Grand Funk Railroad was totally unprepared for Roxy Music: 'Virginia Plain' sank like a stone there. Its addition to the US version of *Roxy Music* (sandwiched between 'If There Is Something' and '2 H.B.') accomplished nothing save to disrupt the album's immaculate running order. That the US track sequencing supplanted the UK original on subsequent pressings worldwide was a piece of aesthetic vandalism not corrected until the 2022 vinyl-reissue program.

**'Virginia Plain'** (Ferry)

One of history's great Pop Art statements is also one of its great pop songs. That buzzing, revving sound, insistent but mixed low, is what precisely? Guitar? Synthesizer? Spaceship? It's Mackay's oboe, as a matter of fact. But it doesn't matter, really, because when all the other instruments spring to life and Ferry howls 'Make me a deal and make it straight', we're off on a three-minute joyride to nowhere anyone had yet been. The speed is breakneck, and the lyrics begin as a self-referential account of the band's signing: 'All signed and sealed, I'll take it/To Robert E. Lee I'll show it/I hope and pray he don't blow it'. By then, of course, Robert Lee (a music industry lawyer at Harbottle & Lewis, not the President of the Confederacy, though the confusion can't have helped the single in America) had decidedly *not* blown it, and Roxy were well on their way to validating Chris Blackwell's confidence in releasing a record he didn't particularly like.

Ferry might sing here about trying and trying to make the big time, but to the outside world, it didn't seem like the band were having to try very hard at all, an impression confirmed by the single's musical and commercial success. The lyric is a collage of showbiz fantasy and throwaway imagery that somehow works. Baby Jane Holzer is in Acapulco, the band are flying down to Rio, and flamingos all look the same when you're standing on a midnight blue casino floor. The music is pure effervescence, gurgling, parping, with a Mackay oboe solo and a guitar solo that Manzanera improvised on the spot. The revving motorbike that marks the bridge was a real one, recorded late at night in Piccadilly Circus, and the trick ending never gets old. Contrary to what you can read on the internet, there was no actual cigarette brand called Virginia Plain. It was, rather, the title of a painting of a cigarette packet that Bryan had done at university – Warhol-style Pop Art, but imaginary. (When recently asked by Mick Wall whether Virginia Plain was a cigarette, a laughing Manzanera answered, 'Well, it was a cigarette *packet*'.) This combination of self-citation and window allusions (when something alludes to something else by means of an intermediary allusion), with a gesture towards the worlds of art and fashion, is all very meta – the whole of Roxy's imaginary world is already here, not in embryo, but fully formed. It's no surprise that this opened up exclusive doors.

**'The Numberer'** (Mackay)

We've already noted the parsimony of Roxy's catalogue – no outtakes or radically different drafts of later successes seem to have survived. Most of their contemporaries are nowadays releasing ten-disc archival editions for 50th anniversaries, documenting their every false start, failed experiment and studio doodle. Not so Roxy. What they recorded, they released. But no band gets everything right the first time on every track, and it has never been clear whether Roxy wiped embarrassing takes immediately or simply didn't press record until they knew they had nailed a track. Regardless, it made for impressive quality control.

That, in turn, brings us to the topic of Roxy B-sides, none of which could ever be mistaken for an A-side. Again, there is a shrewdness here and a merciless realism about their own strengths and weaknesses – not a single Roxy B-side would improve the albums by its addition. By the same token, only one of them is the kind of stinker that should've stayed on the cutting room floor (1975's 'Sultanesque': a shrug in musical form). Especially in the earliest years, Roxy's B-sides were mostly instrumentals, usually credited to Mackay. Often, these compositions were just as exciting as the fully formed songs on the albums, but it seems likely that – as here on 'The Numberer' – Ferry found himself unable to write a convincing lyric over someone else's music, so the compromise was to leave it without a vocal. This track is a jumble of contrasting ideas – a beautiful sax solo, crazed guitar, synths and drums, and then a rocking 'n' rolling harmonica solo that Ferry sustains even as the rest of the track deconstructs around him. It's no 'Virginia Plain' (what is?), but if you listen to their B-side instrumentals end-to-end ('The Numberer', 'The Pride And The Pain', 'Hula Kula', 'Your Application's Failed' and 'Sultanesque'), you get an alternative history of Roxy's evolution from talented, half-amateur eccentrics to rock stars, at the top of their game and knowing just exactly how well they play it.

### **'Pyjamarama'** b/w **'The Pride And The Pain' (single)**

Personnel:
Bryan Ferry: voice, piano
John Porter: bass
Andrew Mackay: oboe, saxophone
Phil Manzanera: guitar
Paul Thompson: drums
Eno: synthesizer, treatments
Produced by Chris Thomas
UK release date: February 1973
US release date: not released
Charts: UK: 12, USA: -
Running time: 3:00/4:16

After the huge success of 'Virginia Plain', parts of the UK music press began to dismiss Roxy Music as little more than manufactured hype. This was partly down to snobbery about singles acts, but also resentment that the band managed to retain their strange coterie of art-world dilettantes and proggy musos while simultaneously adding a whole new audience of teens. Ferry – to this day one of the touchiest men in music – was still smarting about this response five years later, when he told the *NME*'s Paul Rambali that he 'came into pop music from a different angle ... That was the cross that I was sort of impaled upon'.

At the time, he sought consolation with a move out of Battersea and into Redcliffe Square, Earl's Court, while the band prepared to consolidate their success with a British tour. Instead, Ferry collapsed and required an emergency tonsillectomy, which meant a couple of months layoff before they could embark on a rescheduled British tour. That was followed by their first trip to America, which was an unmitigated disaster. Their US label Warner Bros. had failed utterly in promoting the first album, which made virtually no impact despite the addition of the surefire 'Virginia Plain'. Even worse, they were now booked to open for the kind of English bands that America liked (Humble Pie, Jethro Tull) and for the Southern rocker Edgar Winter. It would take till *Siren* (1975) for Roxy Music to gain more than a cult audience in the States, and they returned to Britain licking their wounds.

While they commenced work on their next album, Roxy decided to reward their British fans – who'd voted them Best New Band in all the end-of-year music polls – with a new single. 'Pyjamarama' came out in February 1973, backed – like 'Virginia Plain' – with a Mackay composition. Nowhere near as immediate as its predecessor, 'Pyjamarama' couldn't repeat the chart performance of 'Virginia Plain', peaking at a still respectable number 10 after five weeks in the charts. Any disappointment the band might've felt was surely mitigated by the number-four placing of their second album, which was released just weeks after the single.

**'Pyjamarama'** (Ferry)

This is the first song Ferry wrote on guitar and it sounds like it. The strange, not-quite-right guitar chords are amateurish, but they're lent an anticipatory frisson by Thompson's drums, which cascade through the pauses between chords. Then, when the rest of the band come in, the feel changes completely and Ferry starts to sing in a new, slightly weedy tenor. The tonsillectomy seems to have affected his voice so that the very high falsetto he sometimes used on *Roxy Music* was now beyond him. But that was more than compensated by his much-improved vocal control and by the ability of their new producer, Chris Thomas (a one-time *protégé* of George Martin), who captured a far more robust vocal sound than Pete Sinfield had managed. As on 'Virginia Plain', Ferry's lyric is revealed to be nonsense as soon as one subjects it to any scrutiny ('Just boogaloo a rhapsody divine'??), but the words *feel* as if they make sense for the duration of the track, which is what really matters. Also, he still comes up with some very good lines.

> The world may keep us
> Far apart, but
> Up in heaven, angel
> You can have my heart

That's nicely enough turned, yet it's the surprise phrasing – the placement of the 'but' – that's truly winning. And 'How nice if only/We could/Bill and coo' scores a direct hit with its sweetly archaic euphemism for making out.

Overall, the composition can't match the songs on *For Your Pleasure* (for which it was the non-album teaser), but it improves on many first album tics. While still given the Eno treatment, Mackay is permitted a genuinely pretty Motown-esque sax melody. After his opening fireworks, Thompson hustles the whole thing along with an early version of the Burundi beat made popular by Bow Wow Wow in the 1980s. Eno keeps up a one-note staccato pattern on the synthesizer throughout, which manages to juice up the energy of the other instruments, while Manzanera's extended guitar solo – overlain with more Eno noise – is a less-chaotic take on his 'Ladytron' template.

Unreleased in the States (where they got 'Do The Strand' instead, to no commercial avail), 'Pyjamarama' was remixed by Polydor for 1977's *Greatest Hits* in a slightly shortened edit that also toned the aggression of Eno's treatments right down. The original mix – which has been reinstated on all of the many subsequent Roxy retrospectives – is decidedly superior.

**'The Pride And The Pain'** (Mackay)

It's again worth noting just how little unused detritus Roxy left in their wake. Like 'The Numberer', this Mackay-penned instrumental wouldn't improve any of the albums were it included, but it is actually rather nice to hear. We begin with the sound of wind across the dunes, the call of gulls and plovers on the beach, curlews among the rushes. Completely drumless, the track is effectively an oboe exercise with mirroring guitar counterpoint. The rhythm is supplied by the acoustic piano. However, what could've remained Vaughan Williams pastoral turns urban and nasty with three loud whip-crack sound effects and barely decipherable spoken lines that ooze irritation and then discomfort. (Are they lines of film dialogue pilfered from some obscure Western? The accent sounds American.) Without radically changing either the melody or the soundscape, this intrusion shifts the tone dramatically. As much as anything else, the quality of this track and 'The Numberer' makes you wonder why Mackay's two solo albums (*In Search Of Eddie Riff* (1974) and *Resolving Contradictions* (1978)) weren't stronger.

# For Your Pleasure (1973)

Personnel:
Bryan Ferry: voice, keyboards
Andrew Mackay: oboe, saxophone
Eno: synthesizer, tapes
Paul Thompson: drums
Phil Manzanera: guitars
John Porter (Guest artiste): bass
Produced by Chris Thomas and Roxy Music
UK and US release date: March 1973
Charts: UK: 3, USA: 186
Running time: 42:24

In today's music business, if an established artist releases an album every second year, they are regarded as unusually prolific, so one can easily forget the kind of productivity demanded of bands in the late 1960s and early 1970s. The number of Roxy-adjacent releases that appeared in 1973 is really quite staggering, even for a group of hungry young men on the make. In addition to the 'Pyjamarama' single, there was *For Your Pleasure* (March), *Stranded* (November) and its attendant 'Street Life' single, Mackay's deranged sax contribution to Mott the Hoople's *Mott* (July), Eno's *Here Come The Warm Jets* (recorded in September, though released the following February), featuring all of Roxy except for Ferry, and Ferry's *These Foolish Things* (October) with the whole band except for Mackay and the by-then-departed Eno. Even more surprisingly, every one of these releases was first-rate.

But *For Your Pleasure* remains Roxy's great leap forward. The inspired amateurism of *Roxy Music* was still present and correct, but the vision was more precisely articulated, and crucially, the band's skill sets had improved to where they could actually achieve what they intended, rather than just approximate the sounds they heard in their heads. While Thompson's drumming had started out fully formed, the other core musicians had now moved ahead in leaps and bounds. Manzanera's technique is much improved without losing any unpredictability. You can hear Mackay's new mastery of breath control on the sax (he only squawks when he means to), and Ferry's piano playing is less haphazard. All of this gives Eno far more to work with so that he becomes the guiding chaos agent rather than one lunatic among many. Yet the really astonishing development is Ferry's voice. Though he's still nothing like a conventional singer, all the vocal gaucherie is gone, along with the last trace of Geordie vowels. He's yet to perfect the very bottom of his eventual range, but he can now maintain the crooner tone all the way through a song. His falsetto, too, no longer runs ahead of his ability to catch his breath, and he's just starting to use his vibrato as a deliberate mannerism and not a trick for staying in key. It's hard to believe that Roxy had come so far in less than a year, with nothing but a little bit of experience and practice.

And then there's the artwork. Kari-Ann Moller, on the front of *Roxy Music,* did more than anything to demonstrate the breadth of the band's ambitions, but it succeeded because Nick de Ville and Antony Price had the skills to realize Ferry's concept and also because – in 1972 – Ferry still understood art better than music. By the time of *For Your Pleasure*, his musical proficiency was starting to equal his visual proficiency, and the still more elaborate cover concept was carefully goosed to the exact boundary of the ridiculous with the sublime. It's a gatefold. It's wrapped in sumptuous glossy laminate at Ferry's insistence: that kind of expense took foot-stamping on the artist's part. There's model Amanda Lear in full dominatrix pomp, parading a leashed black panther in front of a cityscape as rain-soaked and gleaming as a Ridley Scott movie. Awaiting the supermodel is a limousine and a cheeky chappie chauffeur straight from central casting. But wait, it's not just any cheeky chappie – it's Bryan!! And wouldn't you know it, by the time the album arrived, Bryan and his cover star were indeed stepping out together: the first of many such liaisons between the artiste and his sleeve muses.

Inside the gatefold, the image-making continued – a series of portraits of the band members (but not 'guest artiste' John Porter) holding guitars in full-length action poses against a stark white background. Karl Stoecker's photos are heavily treated, so they look more like painted illustrations. From left to right there's Eno, standing on one foot as if walking out of the picture, peacock feathers sprouting from his jacket's enormous shoulder pads, blue eye shadow and tweezed eyebrows drawing attention to the white expanse of his balding head; Manzanera, bearded, long hair flowing, eyes closed, mouth half open, deep in the reverie of a solo; Ferry, absurd navy bolero jacket with a splash of violet, navy flares over golden moon boots, channelling Elvis' hip shake while looking down at his guitar; Mackay in profile, white silk jacket, silver cooking-foil codpiece and lavender brothel creepers, his classic quiff streaked with shiny highlights, pretending to play some sort of archaic six-string lute. Finally, there's Thompson, three-quarter profile, but looking backwards into the white ground, blue jumpsuit with yellow-piping, black suede thigh-high boots on stacked heels. Each figure is named in an elegant sans-serif font printed vertically at the bottom right of the portrait. It's such an arresting visual that Roxy's most convincing 21st-century heirs, the Scissor Sisters, paid explicit homage to it on the sleeve of their first album.

Expectations were high and, commercially, *For Your Pleasure* exceeded them. It sold 50,000 copies in the UK in its first week, hitting number four in the charts, spending six weeks in the top ten and six months in the top 100. Reviews were universally glowing. Even the habitually peevish Charles Shaar Murray called it a 'staggeringly fine piece of work'.

Having failed to conquer America, the band set out on a European tour, which they purportedly enjoyed. Certainly, their continental fan base was and remains broader and deeper than the American one. But unbeknownst to their growing audience, trouble was brewing in the Roxy ranks. Eno's comfort with the press led many European journalists to describe Roxy as *his* band, which rankled with Ferry, and their onstage competition was bad for everyone. The European tour ended in late May, and their next commitment was the York Festival on 8 July. With rumours of Bryan-vs-Brian friction now circulating in the press, Eno abandoned the stage at York, hoping that would quieten his highly partisan fans and stop them from drowning out Ferry's vocal on 'Beauty Queen'. The gesture failed, neither rescuing the performance nor mollifying Ferry, who informed E.G. that he would no longer work with Eno before jetting off to Greece in a huff. Not for the last time, Ferry's passive aggression had the desired result and spared him any need for actual confrontation. Eno was out, and the future of Roxy seemed terribly uncertain. But Ferry had a more pliant Eno substitute in mind, while Thompson, Mackay and Manzanera reconciled themselves to a new model Roxy while continuing to collaborate with their ousted friend on other projects. Fifty years on, *For Your Pleasure* reliably ends up in best-album lists. Many – including Ferry himself – now regard it as Roxy's peak, although *Stranded* – released mere months after Eno had left the band – has an equal claim to that title.

**'Do The Strand'** (Ferry)
The pinnacle of Roxy Mk I, this would've gone to number one if only they'd released it as a UK single. The high-octane arrangement doesn't waste a note on gratuitous experiments, because 'Do The Strand' is all about the words. 'There's a new sensation', proclaims Ferry and then Mackay's sax blares. 'A fabulous creation'. This danceable solution to teenage revolution is nothing and everything: a fake dance craze that you can – that you, in fact, must – do everywhere. On moonbeams or rainbows (perhaps in a moonage daydream?), at Quaglino's in St. James's, or Mabel's in Scunthorpe – God help you either way. And if you're beginning to get bored with the beguine, then Toulouse-Lautrec up the Strandsky with La Goulue and Lolita in tow. The listener is bewitched by the intelligence of it all, the sense that deeper meaning lurks behind the absurdism. That the music is so compulsive only increases the fascination of the song, while the bridge – an entirely new musical figure carried by the piano, bass and drums, but melodically dominated by Mackay's treated saxophone – isn't so much a pause for breath as a pause for thought. And then they're off again, having had their fill of quadrilles.

There's an essay by Dr. Simon Puxley – easily found on the internet – that demystifies the lyrics of 'Do The Strand' with the same po-faced attention to detail he had brought to his mumbo jumbo on the *Roxy Music* gatefold. Don't go find it. Instead, try to work out all the references yourself because this is the young Ferry at his most surreal and clever, proving that, whenever he felt like it, he could polish the nonsense lyrics of 'Virginia Plain' and 'Pyjamarama' into something worth decoding. Just don't try to make sense of the greatest ever couplet in rock history: 'Rhododendron is a nice flower/Evergreen, it lasts forever'. Bryan Ferry. The man can find the meaning of life in shrubbery.

**'Beauty Queen'** (Ferry)

One of Ferry's most gorgeous vocal showcases starts with an instrumental three-chord passage that prepares you for something entirely different than what you get. You were expecting a reprise of 'Chance Meeting' from Roxy Music? Have an ironic rendition of Perry Como instead, with lyrics that do justice to both the crooner heritage and post-modern irony. This is what flexing looks like – let's play avant-garde, then let's play MOR, and then let's let the lyrics look after themselves.

Valerie, please… believe
It never could work out
The time to make plans
Has passed, faded away

Conventional, forgettable lines. 'Ooo the way you look/Makes my starry eyes shiver'. Much better. Do eyes shiver? Possibly not, but they could. Or if they couldn't, you still know what he means.

One thing we share
Is an ideal of beauty
Treasure so rare
That even devils might care

There, in those slightly ridiculous lines, Ferry takes it over the top. He sings 'ideal of beauty' but then elongates 'rare' with vibrato. What clinches the deal is the play on the may/might distinction – always grammatically muddy in English, already slightly erudite in 1973, and now almost entirely lost. Ferry makes a meal of the linguistic possibilities. Sure, it's possible for the devils to care, but they're not terribly likely to, and so what? To spell out the pedantry, 'may' belongs in the present tense and conveys no sense of whether something will or won't happen. The phrase 'devil may care' illustrates the ambiguity of 'may' in the present tense: the devil doesn't care if something does or doesn't happen. 'Might' is the trickier partner in the pair – perfectly at home in the past tense, playing the role that 'may' does in the present, but also available in the present tense for those moments where a romance language would use the subjunctive (contrary to fact) to indicate something that could happen but probably won't.

In contrast to the singer's 'starry eyes', there are his beloved's:

Your swimming-pool eyes
In sea breezes they flutter
The coconut tears
Heavy-lidded they shed
Swaying palms at your feet
You're the pride of your street

Like most of Ferry's really good early lyrics, this one merits the exegesis it seems to crave. It's positively intertextual. 'Swimming-pool eyes' is good enough, but it foreshadows the 'new pool' of 'In Every Dream Home A Heartache' two songs later, thus souring the romanticism of the present context. 'Sea breezes' also takes one back to the *Roxy Music* track of that name, asking us to remember how 'Now that we are lonely/Time seems to get hard'. And 'flutter' – the lashes on the swimming-pool eyes, or the swaying palms fluttering in the sea breezes, or perhaps both. And then there's 'pride of your street'. Paul Stump – in his pioneering but invariably perverse Roxy book *Unknown Pleasures* – argues that this line grounds the song firmly not in the gilded palaces of which Ferry dreamed but rather in the threadbare yet house-proud Victorian terraces of his youth. It's a rare glimpse of perspicacity on Stump's part. Ferry's beauty queen exists in his and her own imagination in the same way we all – especially when young – magnify the scale of all emotions, good or bad. 'All of my hope and my inspiration/I drew from you'. But alas, 'Life's pattern's drawn in sand'. And so his own and his beloved's soul ships pass each other by, deep in the night, flying 'solo trips to the stars' and 'Gliding so far that the eye cannot follow'. It's a surprisingly downbeat ending to a song as beautiful as its subject is said to be. On any other album, this would be the standout track. But *For Your Pleasure* is so good, so complete in every way, that at least four other tracks surpass it.

**'Strictly Confidential'** (Ferry)

At first, this seems like one of the less consequential tracks on the album. It lacks the immediacy of the up-tempo numbers, the sheer gorgeousness of 'Beauty Queen', or the weirdness of 'The Bogus Man' and the title track. It's also somewhat overwrought. This is as close as Ferry ever came to generic young male angst, though that's mostly evident in his delivery, not the lyric, which is often rather clever: 'Tongue tied with thread of conversation' or 'Until the cloak of evening shadow/Changes to mantle of the dawn' are pretty good stuff. And 'Some things are better left unsaid' might as well have been the mantra of the post-war generation around whom Ferry grew up. Whether it's a suicide note or an exploration of schizophrenia ('Haunting me always are the voices') doesn't really matter because it's the vocals that are make-or-break here. Ferry's singing is always mannered, but here, it's positively histrionic. That said, once you get past the amateur dramatics and concentrate on the music – which is mixed low and murky to fit the mood – you realize that 'Strictly Confidential' is one of Manzanera's finest performances. After the queasy, fey opening, he starts to drop grace notes whenever Ferry pauses for breath, and as the tension winds tighter, these turn into wailing single notes in counterpoint to the vocal lines. One wonders if it was Eno's idea to bury all this musical complexity in a distanced, muffled soundscape. Especially between the closely mic-ed and loud tracks on either side of it, 'Strictly Confidential' sounds like it's reaching you through a heavy fog – all in aid of the mood, of course, and whether one likes that or not is a matter of taste.

**'Editions Of You'** (Ferry)

One of the eternal Roxy songs, 'Editions Of You' has been played on every Roxy tour and every Ferry solo tour for the past half century, which means even the biggest fans may have become a little bit jaded about it. That's a shame, because it retains everything that made Roxy's first incarnation so eye-poppingly, mind-blowingly wonderful. Staccato electric piano earworm, then the drums enter, and the entire band comes thrashing onto the track at volume, in a mix as thick as setting concrete.

> Well I'm here looking through an old picture frame
> Just waiting for the perfect view
> I hope something special will step into my life
> Another fine edition of you
> A pin-up done in shades of blue

So this is love, is it? – a sequence of pin-up girls, all just copies of one another, and viewed with cool detachment like the vintage photo frames that had decorated the portraits in the *Roxy Music* gatefold? Actually, that had indeed become Ferry's life, going out with cover model Amanda Lear as he began his rapid journey from posing ironically as a playboy to being one. (In reality, Eno was decidedly the more sexually voracious of the two, but it was Ferry whose liaisons made the news.)

If that first verse can be read as evidence of Ferry's self-awareness, the second is sharper still:

> Sometimes you find you're yearning for the quiet life
> The country air and all of its joys
> But badgers couldn't compensate at twice the price
> For just another night with the boys, oh yeah

He's anticipating *Country Life* (the fourth Roxy album), foreshadowing his own desire to join the gentry of *Country Life* (the magazine), and also admitting that the working-class life he was bent on rejecting has genuine pleasures: camaraderie, mateship, playing snooker with Teds in seedy clubs up North. The 'badgers' are as potent and unexpected as the potatoes Ferry was planning to grow in 'If There Is Something' – a genius synecdoche for the world of Barbour, Rovers and Wellington boots that Ferry was determined to enter. Four lines, one verse: an entire dissertation on class and its contradictions.

The metaphors and allusions keep coming. Ferry relocates the sirens and their rocks to the Rhine Gorge and the Lorelei, which had for two centuries been a touchstone for Romantic poets and painters. He lets life's chips fall where they may from the roulette wheel of love. All this wordplay, up against a propulsive rhythm, comes so fast that it's hard to follow – so much so that the two instrumental passages are almost a relief, the first a blazing Manzanera gallop, the second a wild Eno box of tricks. And then there's the final breathless rush for the finish line. 'Love me, leave me, do what you will/ Who knows what tomorrow might bring'. It's hard to tell whether this is the confident bravado of someone who knows they'll be just fine come what may, or whether it's instead the gnawing, heart-in-mouth fear that it will all end tomorrow for someone who's had 'too much cheesecake too soon'. The final line provides an answer of sorts. 'Don't let this happen to you', Ferry warns, but it has happened to him, and for the duration of this track at least, he sounds like he's loving it.

**'In Every Dream Home A Heartache'** (Ferry)

Robert Christgau – perhaps the most influential American rock critic of the 1970s and 1980s – calls this 'a song about an inflatable sex doll that's almost not stupid'. Of course, it's so much more than that, but like most of his countrymen, Christgau had little time for Roxy's archly knowing approach to rock music. Proudly alienated but sinister, a raised eyebrow in musical form, 'In Every Dream Home A Heartache' repelled an American critical fraternity that prized authenticity. However any given critic might define authenticity, Roxy were going to be the antithesis of it. That the song's title alludes to a famous Pop Art collage by Ferry's mentor Richard Hamilton just exacerbated the annoyance. (Hamilton's *Just What Is It That Makes Today's Homes So Different, So Appealing* (1956) is now in the city art museum of Tübingen). English critics at the time were more forgiving and, since then, the track has come to be regarded as the key to unlocking the Roxy universe, written about so frequently that it's hard for anyone not to slip into the commonplace and *cliché*.

Briefly (and virtually any book in the bibliography will offer additional comment), the song uses its three vocal and four instrumental sections to essay a commentary on the plasticity of modern consumer culture – plastic in the technical sense of ever-shifting its shape, but also in the modern pejorative sense of cheap, ersatz and disposable. We start with a glowering sax underpinning Ferry's 'In every dream home, a heartache/And every step I take, takes me further from heaven'. 'Is there a heaven?' he asks. Well, he'd like to think so. Then he starts to outline all the mod cons of his mid-century-modern palace – open-plan living, its comforts essential from the bell-push to the faucets (and note that vogue-ish American term for the British tap). But what to do in today's ever-so-appealing home? 'Better pray there', though for what, exactly, is unclear.

Part two is the sex-doll section, the mail-order baby, the perfect companion with deluxe vinyl skin (pronounced as French *de luxe* to rhyme with English 'looks'). He blew up this ungrateful lover's body, and then she blew his mind. Suddenly, Manzanera erupts into a scorching solo that build to a crescendo, while Eno turns all the knobs up to 11 and Ferry wails about all love's heartaches. With Thompson battering his drums like a madman and Manzanera still in full flight, Eno fades into a silence that lasts eight seconds – long enough to make you think it's all over – and then fades back into a coda as he pushes all the instrumental tracks into the weird, distorted noise with which the song, and the album side, end. The music's sonic violence enunciates the stifled emotion that the numbed vocals cannot.

Some will hear misogyny in these lyrics – disdain for all those many ungrateful lovers who've been rendered unnecessary by a life-size immortal, a 'disposable darling', who can blow your mind just as well as a real woman. Others will hear despair, a mind blown apart by the realization that a commercial object cannot love you back. However perfect a companion this female facsimile might be, and however much the singer can't throw her away, she remains a 'plain-wrapper baby', a mute testament to his romantic failure. Either way you choose to hear it, the song is The Beatles' 'Can't Buy Me Love', but cold and heartless, all optimism sucked dry.

### **'The Bogus Man'** (Ferry)

If you want to argue that *For Your Pleasure* is *not,* in fact, Roxy's greatest album, exhibit A is 'The Bogus Man' – nine minutes and 22 seconds of a cyclically repeating guitar riff, stalking bass and drums, and Hammer-horror oboe. The stalker figure from the first album's 'Ladytron' reappears here in a more literal guise, 'scratching at your throat'. The lyric is slight, and the vocal concludes a good five minutes before the song does. Minor variations of melody play out over minor variations in rhythm, and then the whole thing just stops dead. It's the song Eno cites as evidence for the experimental promise of early Roxy that lost out to Ferry's commercial instinct. Perhaps so, but the band reintroduced it to the live set for their 50th-anniversary tour in a tighter and more song-like arrangement, proving that a melody had been lurking in there all along.

The early 1970s birthed a lot of very long, very pointless tracks, from prog rock operatics to mind-numbing blues jams, to the handful of Stones and Zeppelin epics that transcend that kind of pretension and idiocy. This is like none of that. It's Can, it's Kraftwerk, it's John Cage. And it goes on for bloody ever.

### **'Grey Lagoons'** (Ferry)

A bit of froth, but a pleasant one, held over from the previous year, and known on its demo version (a rare survival, that) as 'The Bogus Man Part II' – a perverse joke, one assumes, as nothing could be further from that motorik workout. 'Grey Lagoons' has a cinematic piano accompaniment, lush and mixed loud as on 'Beauty Queen', while Ferry pours out nonsense imagery about silver starfish and honeymoons, satin teardrops and velvet lights. Also, 'Morning sickness on Friday nights', which doesn't sound very nice at all. After that, broken partings make strange goodbyes for all the hopeless cases with fake alibis. None of it hangs together, certainly not the lyric, but none of it needs to. It's like the theme to an imaginary movie: you find yourself painting pictures in your head, and it's unclear whether it's the lyric, the vocal or the overall atmospherics that are guiding that mental paintbrush. Yet it's in the extended instrumental passages in the middle that the genius actually lies. As Ferry holds the last note of his vocal, Mackay launches a frenzied, dance-friendly sax solo, which Ferry then interrupts with a syncopated harmonica bridge that gives way to one of Manzanera's lightning, chordless solos. Then two of the three opening verses repeat themselves, and it ends in a ridiculously extended 'la-goo-oo-oo-oo-oo-oo-ns' that ranges beyond a full octave. It's quick, it's fun, it's optimistic, and it has all the brio and vivacity of 'Editions Of You', lacking only its incandescent wit.

**'For Your Pleasure'** (Ferry)

Whereas 'Grey Lagoons' passed in the blink of a dizzy eye, the title track unfolds in such stately leisure that its almost seven minutes feel considerably longer. Ah, you say, *this* is the actual 'Bogus Man' part two. Mercifully, it is not. Whereas fair-minded listeners can hate 'The Bogus Man' fair-mindedly, it requires a sort of curdled ill-humour to dislike 'For Your Pleasure', which is clearly the one and only perfect merger of Ferry and Eno's aesthetics. Electric piano, guitar, bass, drums, what have you – every instrument is a sound effect. But those effects are weird and disconcerting, the drums and piano that underpin most of the opening, lyrical segment sounding absolutely huge, as if echoing off the walls of a large empty room. At first, they punctuate weary lyrics that belong to a much older man than Ferry was at the time:

In the morning
Things you worried about
Last night
Will seem lighter
I hope things
Will turn out right

But this is not 'Editions Of You', nor even 'Beauty Queen', where the hopes, the mights, and the mays offer the potential for both brightness and darkness, success and failure, where the outcome remains uncertain.

Not so here. The hope that things will turn out right is a hope forlorn. 'You watch me walk away', because what else can one do when confronted with the final failure that is death: Ferry is addressing an 'old man' who can only be his future self, a future self who is watching the present self walk away. But as we all know, present self will eventually be future self and we'll ultimately need to say goodbye to both of them – or perhaps not goodbye but rather 'ta-ra', that Northern variant of 'ta-ta', which Ferry here enunciates without a trace of Northern accent.

As his first 'Ta-ra' echoes, the instruments creating the musical palate begin to dissolve and soon drift off into an ambient soup that is somehow comforting and pastoral while obviously an aural meditation on – or representation of – the slow submersion into mortality that the lyric had already telegraphed. By the end, there's nothing left but an electronic haze built from bits of sound you can't really identify. Yet how seriously one is meant to take any of it had already been put in doubt at the start of the track, which announces itself as 'part false, part true, like anything': the entire story of Roxy Music in one epigram.

## Stranded (1973)

Personnel:
Bryan Ferry: voice, piano
Andrew Mackay: oboe, saxophone, treatments
Paul Thompson: drums, timpani
Phil Manzanera: guitar, treatments
Eddie Jobson: violin, synthesizer, keyboards
Johnny Gustafson: bass
Produced by Chris Thomas
UK release date: November 1973
US release date: May 1974
Charts: UK: 1, USA: 186
Running time: 41:06

Exit Eno, enter Eddie Jobson – ten years Ferry's junior and also from the Northeast, where his and Ferry's sisters had been flatmates. Jobson was a musical prodigy who'd played with Curved Air and who Ferry initially lined up as a jack-of-all-trades for his first solo album. Among the various things Jobson had going for him was his youth, which Ferry correctly foretold would make him unlikely to challenge the singer's supremacy within the band. As importantly, Jobson was not brought in as an equal partner. Though he was presented as a full member of the band in the liner notes and on the sleeves of all three Roxy Music records he contributed to, Jobson was a salaried player. To his advantage, that meant he didn't have to take on any of the band's still-substantial recording debts, but it also deprived him of any royalties on arrangements. To this day, he cannot suppress some bitterness when he's asked to speak about Roxy.

But in the moment, the conditions of Jobson's hiring kept Mackay and Manzanera (still Eno's close friends) on board. Also, the band needed someone on synthesizer to fill their Eno-shaped hole, and Jobson could do that despite his studied musicianship being more conventional than Eno's autodidacticism.

He would also add his violin to the sonic mix, as he had done to Ferry's groundbreaking solo cover of 'A Hard Rain's A-Gonna Fall', and contribute more tutored piano arrangements than Ferry could himself.

The latter half of 1973 was when large parts of the mercurial UK music press turned definitively against Roxy, or rather, against Ferry, whom they blamed (correctly) for Eno's departure and whose increasingly frosty interview habits were taken as a provocation. Reading these pieces in chronological order half a century later, it's clear that Ferry and the press had a mutually corrosive relationship – the more touchy he got, the more the press goaded him. The *NME,* in particular, relished the opportunity to mangle his name: Byron Ferrari (obvious, appropriate even), Brawn Fairy (merely silly) or Biriyani Ferret (sublime, almost poetic).

To break in Roxy Mk II, the band embarked on a short British tour in the late summer, after which they went right back into the studio to put down a collection of songs that would, for the first time, include co-writing credits for Manzanera and Mackay. The general consensus at the time was that Ferry's playboy image was going to get the better of the music. With its release in November, *Stranded* proved the critics all wrong. For this listener, it is Roxy's finest hour, and no one would now deny that it's neck-and-neck with *For Your Pleasure* for first place. Eno has long declared it his favourite Roxy album with a magnanimity that at least seems genuine. Sceptics were silenced. Charles Shaar Murray and Ian Macdonald – discerning and acerbic creatures who rarely agreed on anything – proclaimed *Stranded* to be a masterpiece in *Melody Maker* and the *NME,* respectively. For the first time, the band pulled a single from an album, and 'Street Life' duly entered the top ten.

The album did even better, peaking at number one and eventually selling respectably in America, where Warner Bros. had dropped the band and Atco had picked them up. The gatefold cover was as carefully constructed as ever, though it has aged rather less well than the first two. *Playboy* centrefold Marilyn Coles, stretched full-length on what is meant to be a jungle floor, was intended to look ravishing but instead looks ravished in a torn red frock, soaking wet. It might have worked better had the jungle background been given the same attention as the model's makeup. Though it looks impossibly sexist now, and pushed against the boundaries of good taste at the time, contemporaries would perhaps have seen in it the exotic glamour that Ferry surely intended.

The album's success comes down to the sky-high quality of the songs. The ideas in 'A Song For Europe' and 'Mother Of Pearl' could've been harvested for half a dozen songs and would've been by any normal band, while the other six tracks are very nearly as good. The playing is impeccable; everyone has mastered his instrument without losing the imaginative spark of the initially self-taught. More importantly, no one is showing off, not even Ferry. Or rather, they're all showing off as an ensemble, with no one trying to monopolise the spotlight. Epic self-restraint seems a contradiction in terms, but that's precisely what Roxy pull off on *Stranded* for the first and only time. Also, the record sounds huge, expansive, and mixed loudly, but with a spacious sonic field so you can easily pick out individual elements in the mix. For that, producer Chris Thomas probably deserves credit. He had learned how to work with this band in all their experimental glory on the previous album, where the sound – the mic placement, the loudness, the density of the mix – changed from track to track. In contrast, *Stranded* sounds all of a piece, a coherent sonic statement to match the musical one. Roxy were to refine and consolidate this approach on the much denser *Country Life* – a fine album indeed – but they would never again scale the peaks of *Stranded*.

**'Street Life'** (Ferry)

The album opens with some distorted shimmying noise, said to be the sound of a crowd in a Moroccan market, though you'd be hard-pressed to identify it as such. There's no mistaking the propulsive energy that powers the track forward, however: a wall of noise composed of guitar, strings, sax and some highly agile bass from John Gustafson, who would play on the next two Roxy albums as well.

Like 'Editions Of You' on *For Your Pleasure*, 'Street Life' is a reflection of Ferry's ambivalence about the choices people make in trying to move out of the class into which they were born. Before, it was 'Badgers couldn't compensate'; here, it's 'Education is an important key, yes/But the good life's never won by degrees, no'. Now hang on a moment there – strictly speaking, Bryan's good life was indeed won by degrees (a degree from Newcastle, to be precise, which gave him the skills and vocabulary to articulate a vision that could never have borne fruit in his pit village). One could also understand 'degrees' as 'stages, increments', and here, too, Bryan's good life was won by stages, half measures during those first three thankless years in London. The press might have believed the legend of his exploding into the high life fully formed, but he wasn't altogether happy with the result:

The sidewalk papers gutter-press you down
All those lies can be so unkind
They can make you feel like you're losing your mind

Ambivalence – one comes to accept – is a very Bryan Ferry emotion, even when disguised by something as surprising as 'gutter-press' used as a verb.

The song is perfectly structured to build tension, from the initial eruption through a short, controlled bridge, before the final three verses take off and press two iconic chocolate brands into the lyric's service without so much as a nod or a wink.

Weekend starts Friday soon after eight
Your jet black magic helps you celebrate
You may be stranded if you stick around
And that's really something

The song finishes on a single note, shimmering into the middle distance without resolving into an actual ending. You can't always get what you want, the Rolling Stones had said. Yes, you can, Ferry replies, and to your cost.

**'Just Like You'** (Ferry)

Perennially underrated, even by the band, and very rarely performed, this is one of Ferry's most affecting love songs. It's an elaborate meditation on the mutability of life and love, with an abundance of evocative similes. Buttercups and daisies wither and fade, weather blows hot or cold, alchemy turns iron into gold. Ferry moulds his phrasing to the melody in challenging ways, as in 'Time conquers inno-/-cence, pride takes a fall'. As he ramps up the intensity, his vocals are tracked in octaves to create a slightly off-pitch harmony as he professes himself to be walking through the streets while hopelessly grounded, in reverie over lost loves.

The arrangement is simple, piano-led, Mackay and Manzanera largely relegated to sonic embellishment, although the latter delivers a soaring, deliciously melancholy solo after a vocal bridge that takes the mood into much darker territory than before. When the vocals return, as Manzanera holds the solo's last note suspended, Ferry extends the metaphor of change into the world of fashion, 'when the latest creation is last year's fab rave'. His thought patterns, he declares, have become hazy and he wonders whether lady luck, 'old and sage', will shine on him. One tends to be sceptical when Ferry aims for sincerity, and one's scepticism is often justified when he rapidly undercuts his own sentiment. Not here:

You see, I know it sounds crazy
But what can I do?
I've fallen head over heels
Over you

Perhaps so, but, alas for him, the object of his love is in continual metamorphosis:

Chameleon colour
All phases of moon
The shifting of planets
And leopard spots too
As destiny wills it
So seasons will change
Just like you

Head over heels he may be, but although just for this moment she loves him back, it surely can't last. The piano rounds things off on a rising note of interrogation, and it's done. Ferry went on to play the hopeless lover for so long that it became a pallid, attenuated gesture, but this early variation on his enduring theme is as close as he ever came to perfecting it.

**'Amazona'** (Manzanera, Ferry)

Manzanera's first co-writing credit is – as one might expect – musically distinguishable from Ferry's compositions. There's a funky, syncopated rhythm, while the bass from John Gustafson is rubbery and propulsive as it slinks around the edges of Manzanera's elaborate guitar lines. These are frequently spectacular, and it's difficult to tell how much is achieved by the guitarist's dexterity and his effects pedals and how much by Jobson imitating Eno's sonic disruptions.

Either way, Ferry again proves his knack for delivering more-or-less nonsense lyrics as if they mean something. 'From Arizona to Eldorado/Sure is a mighty long way' might well be true and is certainly unfalsifiable. The only interest of 'Sometimes paradise/Around your corner lies' is the striking anastrophe (the words deliberately reversing normal syntax), and that's about the height of the lyric because this one really is about the music. You can hear the impact of Manzanera's itinerant childhood in Latin America – a bounce and a lightness of touch that counters the portentousness of the Ferry track that follows. It's the muse the guitarist would tap into on his fine solo album *Diamond Head* (1975) and bring to a long and successful career as a producer in the Spanish-speaking world.

**'Psalm'** (Ferry)

A divisive track, this. Pop and rock are just fine with displays of religious fervour as long as said religion is either esoteric (Kabbalah) or exotic (Sufism) and preferably non-Western. But Christianity makes people – and critics especially – more than a little bit squeamish. So, on its initial release, 'Psalm' was passed over in silence by the most enthusiastic reviewers or, in a handful of cases, was flagged as the sole problematic track on the album. That it is very long and builds slowly probably didn't help. Ferry had worked on it for a long time, presumably knowing that it wasn't going to be the easiest sell. But back then, he was still testing his own limits as a songwriter, and penning a convincing hymn was a new challenge. As long as you accept that parameter, he clearly succeeds.

He starts by comparing love to a new piece of clothing one tries on ('The fit and the cut, your friends to impress') before suggesting we try out our god by trying on his coat ('A mantle most fine/Myriad colours'), continuing the fashion metaphor and perhaps indicting the various musicians whose dalliances with self-actualisation and exotic religiosity were such a feature of the early 1970s. And then he pivots:

His harmony thine
'Believe in me'
Once seemed a good line
Now belief in Jesus
Is faith more sublime

The music starts to get a bit more emphatic, Thompson becomes more assertive, and Manzanera's little guitar commentaries get trickier. It's probably right about here that contemporary critics started to get uncomfortable – he can't mean it, can he? But he rather sounds like he does. And it keeps coming. 'I'll stand at his gate/I'll wait for his sign'. 'His quiet waters/Will never ever run dry'. 'I'll walk in his garden/When it's my time'. 'He leads me to paradise/A mountain so high'. Ferry draws out that 'high', working his way up a whole octave as we pass into the instrumental section where the band unleash a quiet storm. Ferry takes a soaring harmonica solo in the foreground, Mackay's oboe starts blowing New Orleans style, and the London Welsh Male Choir launches wordless vocals so low in the mix that you don't notice it at first and instead wonder why the sound has become fuller. As the harmonica solo ends, Manzanera gathers up the melody, picking at single strings.

Then Ferry roars back in with 'Don't be afraid/Just treasure his word'. It's places like this that you realize how quickly he had improved as a singer, and how much he'd learned while recording his solo album of covers. Gospel clichés proceed to tumble forth as the choir gradually rises through the mix, and Mackay turns on the theatrics. 'Some day his house will be my home/ For evermore'. He keeps repeating that 'For evermore', vibrato now definitely intentional, as the choir finally becomes identifiable as choir, and Ferry even allows himself to improvise a little, with a finger-clicking exclamation of 'Hey!'.

The whole thing fades out with all the musical elements still in full swing, and I'd love to know how long the original recording continued for. Ferry achieves what he set out to achieve, and the band back him to the hilt. In a German television performance of the song, Ferry looks blank rather than fervent, and you suspect that this really was just a songwriting exercise for him. That said, whether he meant it or not, and whether *they* meant it or not, the entire ensemble sounds as if they were having the time of their lives on this recording. There's a real human joy in that, which is entirely independent of any god you care to name.

**'Serenade'** (Ferry)

The triumphant curtain raiser on one of the best album sides ever, 'Serenade' is the perfect marriage of propulsive music and the best kind of Ferry lyric. Backwards vocal reverb fades up into Ferry's opening salvo: 'Darkness falls 'round your window pane', but the light burning there is a mere smouldering flame, passion extinguished. 'Is it the end of another affair?/An open engagement with gloom?'. Probably, but perhaps there's hope: 'Or will you be smiling/When the sun conjures up/A broken spell?/*Au claire de lune*'. It's a neat conceit to have the rising sun conjure up both the refrain of an 18th-century French folk song about moonlight and also Paul Verlaine's 1869 poem of that title, made famous in Claude Debussy's piano arrangement. Alas, Ferry and the beloved with whom he'd shared 'a summer enchantment by an old mill stream' have now passed 'from courtly love to costly game'. It's a surprisingly mature and even clinical acknowledgement that infatuations always end and that their endings cause great pain if all there ever was to them was the infatuation itself. Manzanera's guitar then gets space for an economical solo before the piano comes to the fore on a bridge that reveals that Ferry's beloved is indeed finally leaving. As the primary melody resumes, all that's left is to beg her to hide away in the 'Sacred hours, saved from yesterday'.

The last two verses are the kind of actual poetry that marks *Stranded* out as Roxy's best album:

Boo-hoo willows
Weep around you still
Mirror reflections of dew
But waterfall pages
Of an open book
Could shower new horizons soon

Call the tune
Would you swoon
As I croon
Your serenade?

Very few pop lyrics survive commission to cold hard print, a point proven by Faber & Faber's admirable series of books presenting lyrics (by Jarvis Cocker, Kate Bush, Neil Tennant, Robert Wyatt, et al.) as if they were poems, and also by most of the post-*Siren* content of Ferry's *Lyrics* (2022). But this bit? It scans, its internal rhymes and half-rhymes transcend *cliché*, and the jumble of imagery repays close reading. Ferry writes 'Boo-hoo' for weeping but brings 'weep' back in as a verb. The various watery permutations – tears, dew, showers and cascades – ring all the changes on the liquid vocabulary. Hold a book sideways, let it fall open, and you can indeed imagine its pages as a kind of waterfall. It's a bravura performance, topped off by Ferry's dropping harmonic position on each of the closing lines: the 'croon' is so far below his normal range that it would previously have been beyond him and he would have gone flat. Here, he's able to pull it off. You'd think this was the peak of his powers were it not for the tracks that follow, which are better still.

**'A Song For Europe'** (Mackay, Ferry)

This is Mackay's first co-write, and it would be wrong not to point out its striking parallels to George Harrison's 'While My Guitar Gently Weeps'. But as with The Jam of all people ('Start!' and The Beatles' 'Taxman'), Mackay and Ferry improve on The Beatles. Minor-key piano stalks the soundscape, played by Jobson with vastly more sophistication than Ferry could have brought to it. Manzanera and Gustafson add ballast, and Mackay's sax haunts the choruses and dominates the bridge.

Here as I sit
At this empty café
Thinking of you
I remember
All those moments
Lost in wonder
That we'll never
Find again

Ferry comes on all *chanteur*: Yves Montand or a Mandraxed Jacques Brel. 'Though the world is my oyster/It's only a shell full of memories': absurd, yet also a perfect subversion of clichéd idiom. 'Here by the Seine/Notre-Dame casts a long lonely shadow' places the singer explicitly in the continental context, the sophistication of which he always strove to inhabit, while slyly sending up the Eurovision song contest. 'Through silken waters/My gondola glides/And the bridge, it sighs' captures the essence of Ferry's appeal, as he takes a lyric that is risible on the face of it and loads it with so much simulated emotion that you're forced both to believe in him and laugh out loud at the same time. Between each of the quiet piano-led verses, there are the impassioned choruses – variations on 'There's no more time for us/Nothing is there/For us to share/But yesterday' – during which Mackay cuts loose with his best sax-playing ever, and Thompson gins up the excitement with great, crashing fills.

If it ended after just two or so minutes, it would already have been a classic. But 'A Song For Europe' goes on to 5:47, amping up the drama with one of rock's most striking conceptual conceits – while Mackay goes berserk low in the mix, Ferry recites the entire chorus in Latin translated by Simon Puxley, after which they do it all again in French, Ferry belting out the lyrics like Colm Wilkinson in *Les Miserables* – 'Touts ces moments/Perdus dans l'enchantement/Qui ne reviendront/Jamais': the English chorus made French. 'Oh, jamais, jamais, jamais, jamais': Never, never, never again will they recover their enchanted moment. It all finishes with Ferry whistling, fading out, a despondent *flaneur* vanishing into the Paris darkness with only his cigarette for company.

In concert, the band gave 'A Song For Europe' a showboating coda – all thrilling piano, climactic drums and Mackay wailing away centre stage. But the delicacy of the studio version, with every instrument placed flawlessly in the mix, is a triumph of Chris Thomas' production. It is Roxy *in excelsis*.

**'Mother Of Pearl'** (Ferry)
Exploding with a blast of Manzanera noise and multi-tracked Ferrys talking over one another, 'Mother Of Pearl' is two songs in one. The furious metallic roar of its first two minutes give way to an easygoing, syncopated stroll for the remaining five, during which the backing track gets ever more baroque,

and new instrumentation comes in before stopping dead for an *a cappella* coda and another trick ending. The song's two parts – though completely dissimilar – perfect one another. Without the opening firestorm, the rest would become aimless and enervating. (This was proven in 2023 when Ferry finally released the nine-minute nightclub-funk version he'd cooked up circa 1992 for the ultimately abandoned *Horoscope* album.)

A lot has been written about 'Mother Of Pearl', not least about its audaciously duelling Ferrys, their exhortations to each other flitting between channels: 'Turn the lights down/*Way down low*/Turn up the music/*Hi as fi can go*'. This last line, once you've decoded it, has the frisson of the unexpected that you expect from an on-form Ferry. Then the Ferrys start shouting at one another, angry and hostile:

> What's your number
> Never you mind
> Take a powder
> Wait a minute what's that coming round the corner?
> Have you a future?
> No no no no
> Yes

Manzanera carries his solo to a wild conclusion over 30 seconds, and as it fades, a piano begins a gentle rhythm, an organ rings, and then Gustafson and Thompson roll us into the languid rhythm that will carry us right to the end.

Garry Mulholland – discussing Roxy's *Greatest Hits* (1977) in his *Fear of Music* – nailed a core part of the Ferry aesthetic. His analysis of 'Mother Of Pearl' (included on that compilation despite the song never having been a single, let alone a hit) remains unsurpassed:

> Was Johnny Rotten – a huge Ferry fan – sourcing 'Mother Of Pearl''s 'Have you a future?/No, no, no, NO!!!' for 'God Save The Queen'? Ferry answers his own question with the most sinister 'yes' in pop history – whatever future he's seen, you suspect that it is heartless and cruel and that his 'yes' is his own desire to join the landed gentry, which he did. This is, after all, the only UK rock star I can think of who's always admitted that he's a conservative.

Mulholland's insight builds on what Caroline Coon (see the *Siren* entry) observed in Melody Maker about Ferry's ambition to move out of the working class of his birth, first into the ostensibly classless world of the *avant-garde*, then into a sort of pantomime version of aristocracy, before securing – with his marriage to Lucy Helmore – a passport into the lower reaches of the real thing.

Like 'Editions Of You' or 'Street Life', and behind all the puns and clever lyrics, on 'Mother Of Pearl', Ferry concedes that his raw ambition to get ahead comes at a real cost but that he's willing to pay that painful price.

I've been up all night (again?)
Party time wasting is too much fun
Then I step back thinking of life's inner meaning
And my latest fling

Staying up all night wasting time on endless flings: these are the very meaning of life. But how much meaning can there be in waste? Is there actually anything there? As Ferry says, 'If you're looking for love in a looking-glass world/It's pretty hard to find', but what he doesn't tell us is whether this is the type of looking glass that you can – like Alice – step through, or whether it's a plain old mirror that will keep reflecting you back at yourself no matter how hard you stare.

The lyrics on 'Mother Of Pearl' are as dense as in 'Do The Strand', with phrases and juxtapositions that are so individually striking ('serpentine sleekness', 'Feather bed quilted, faced with silk, softly stuffed eiderdown', 'Your choker provokes a picture cameo') that they don't really need to cohere. His mother of pearl is a 'lonely dreamer', 'so-so semi-precious', a 'submarine lover in a shrinking world'. And the good life is definitely out there in 'Canadian Club love' and 'filigree fancy', while naturally, 'everyone's ideal' is 'a place in the country'.

As the song progresses, the band and producer Thomas over-stuff the music to match the silken, over-stuffed lyric. By the end, there's Mackay's baritone saxophone, Manzanera's two guitar parts, a piano and a xylophone. Then, as this whole glorious noise comes to a dead stop, *a cappella* Ferrys sing, 'Oh Mother of Pearl/I wouldn't trade you for another girl' four times. It catches you off guard every time he picks back up again, wrong-footing you entirely when the final repetition segues immediately into the next track. Ferry's music has always been a 'search for perfection'. 'Mother Of Pearl' is the closest he ever came to finding it.

**'Sunset'** (Ferry)

Behind the final 'girl' in the coda to 'Mother Of Pearl', a diffident piano announces the changed mood of 'Sunset': crepuscular and valedictory, the sense of an ending suspended in the air. The languorous tempo never quickens and, as on the previous two tracks, more and more instrumentation slips in to complement the bowed contrabass of Chris Lawrence and Ferry's warm-toned piano. Lyrically, 'Sunset' is Ferry using one of his key techniques – setting himself a theme and then trying to exhaust its possibilities, using the English language's unusual wealth of synonyms to work through every thematic variation he can conjure. Where

'Serenade' opened this album side with the sun-evoking 'Au claire de lune', 'Sunset' closes it with that 'slow-burning star sinking low'. Ferry's phrasing is ingenious: 'Heaven knows where you go/Out of sight's out of mind's eye, no' is easily heard as 'Out of sight's out of mind, I know', which works just as well with the following:

Ah, such a shame you must leave
All day long you were a friend to me
Still the Moon's company
Until morning when larks will sing

The melancholy pastoral evokes the daily cycle of light and dark and the creatures whose behaviours punctuate it. But it also recalls such cultural touchstones of Ferry's childhood as the novels of Flora Thompson's *Lark Rise* trilogy. In contrast, 'Horizon's appointment you'll keep/For sunswept flamingos must sleep' points inevitably back to 'Virginia Plain' and its flamingos that look the same – a piece of self-reference that underscores Ferry's musical progress from Pop Art to Rococo.

The bridge, on which Thompson begins to make a gentle, rhythmic presence felt, is still mostly piano and bass but with tinkling triangle that continues to underpin the vocals as they resume. 'Why are you sad?/Do you disapprove?' Ferry asks.

How we've wasted our time
Sunset
End of my day
My decline

Any hint of maudlin self-pity is banished by:

Postscript you trace, colours the sky
Red-letter light fades
Is filed away
Sunburst fingers you raise
One last sigh of farewell
Goodbye

The descending glide of 'decline' into the ascending 'postscript' is an especially fine vocal effect, as is the rhetorical figure in the first couplet, where 'postscript' serves first as an object, then as the subject of the respective verbs. Indeed, these two final verses, and especially the superb 'sunburst fingers', recognizably paint the optical effect of the sun's last rays hitting atmospheric water just before it drops below the horizon – a warm glow, out of which tendrils seek the empyrean.

Meticulously crafted it may be, but 'Sunset' reminds us that Ferry's best lyrics can succeed as poetry. That's a rare thing, and it bears celebration.

**Related Material**
**'Street Life'** b/w **'Hula Kula' (single)**
Personnel: as above
UK release date: November 1973
US release date: not released
Charts: UK: 9, USA: -
Running time: 3:29/2:40

**'Street Life'**
'Pyjamarama' was the last stand-alone single Roxy released until 'Jealous Guy' in 1981. Beginning with the *Stranded* album and its 'Street Life' single, the band drew their singles from albums, generally adding a non-album B-side. The single version of 'Street Life' is identical to the album version.

**'Hula Kula'**
Roxy's third B-side was Manzanera's first composition for the band. More frothy than Mackay's 'The Numberer' and 'The Pride And The Pain', it's a Hawaiian affair, all twangy island lead guitar over a strummed acoustic that keeps time in the absence of drums. There's a bit of Ferry whistling near the start, some near-subliminal wordless vocals underpinning the guitar melody, and, towards the end, some movie-style dialogue. All told, it's pleasant enough to hear but not really good enough to put on intentionally.

## Country Life (1974)

Personnel:
Bryan Ferry: voice, keyboards
Andrew Mackay: oboe, saxophone
Paul Thompson: drums
Phil Manzanera: guitar
Edwin Jobson: strings, synthesizer, keyboards
John Gustafson: bass
Produced by Roxy Music and John Punter
UK release date: November 1974
US release date: January 1975
Charts: UK: 3, USA: 37
Running time: 41:25

Each of the previous three albums had been a significant development from its predecessor – a reinvention of who the band was and what its music meant – but *Country Life* was Roxy's consolidation album. It is transparently the work of the same band that had made *Stranded* the year before, both literally (John Gustafson was the first bassist to last from one album to the next) and figuratively. All the elements that made *Stranded* a triumph remain here, redeployed in a much heavier and denser mix. *Country Life* doesn't peak quite as high, perhaps – nothing is quite as frantic and impenetrable as 'Street Life', nothing as hazily beautiful as 'Sunset', and of course nothing can touch the perfection of 'Mother Of Pearl', not even 'The Thrill Of It All', though it is by any measure one of Roxy's finest tracks. But there is also nothing as divisive as 'Psalm' or incongruous as 'Amazona'.

Everything is of a piece, Mackay and Manzanera having gained a technical mastery that evaded the early band, while Jobson's contribution is noticeably more prominent. Ferry's vocal control rarely fails him, and while his lyrics have become more literal, that doesn't yet compromise the quirky Pop Art collage that originally distinguished his songwriting. John Punter was an astute choice of producer. He seems to have understood that a group of musicians this accomplished, playing at the top of their game, could've spun rapidly out of control, egos flashing and competing for prominence, so he reins in any hint of showboating. The mix rewards concentration, and even after decades of listening, there remain surprises in the way the different instruments interact. Roxy would return to Chris Thomas and his much more airy – one might say more lenient – production for the subsequent *Siren*, but Punter's contribution here is nearly the equal of George Martin during The Beatles' peerless middle period.

Then, because it's Roxy we're talking about, there's the cover: *that* cover. Ferry cared (and cares) about image so much that with a slight nudge in the wrong direction, his image-making risks overwhelming his music. There's no danger of that here, but still… *that* cover. A pair of very womanly women –

the foliage of suggestive lushness, the lingerie that hides nothing. Yes, there is the fairly obvious play on the Barbour aesthetics of the magazine *Country Life*, right down to the font chosen for the title. But even at the time, the whiff of amateur pornographer was inescapable, and American and Australian prudes were duly scandalized. (American copies were swiftly clad in green shrink-wrap, and later pressings got a sleeve with just the greenery, the models excised.) The exploitative aspect of the cover is somewhat redeemed by the fact that Constanze Karoli and Eveline Grünwald (respectively sister and girlfriend of Can's Michael Karoli) look the way real human beings do when they take their clothes off – there's no trace of the sculpted catwalk fantasies to which Ferry's album covers became wedded after *Flesh + Blood* (1980). What's more, Ferry gave Karoli and Grünwald a cover credit for the German translation of the lyrics of the penultimate verse of 'Bitter Sweet'. So, an aesthetic misstep, but taken in good faith.

One could make a good case for *Country Life* as the definitive Roxy Mk II album if not necessarily the best. But the band itself seems to have had rather less affection for it. While the album had a muscular place in the set of their 1975 and 1976 tours, only 'Out Of The Blue' was selected for the *Viva! Roxy Music* compilation (1976), and it's also the only track to have maintained its place in the live repertoire long-term. After the album was recorded but shortly before its release, Ferry did a pair of very expensive high-profile solo shows at the Royal Albert Hall, and, tellingly, it was there that he debuted two songs from *Country Life* ('Casanova' and 'A Really Good Time'). Mackay had already parlayed his Roxy success into a modestly successful solo LP, Manzanera was about to follow suit, and both were prolific contributors to other artists' recordings, most notably albums by Eno, John Cale and Nico. The whole band had also become financially comfortable by this time, which meant they needed the album-tour-album grind less than they previously had. In short, Roxy had made it. The cracks weren't yet showing, certainly not the way they would after *Siren* came out. But looking back, you can see the signs of the band beginning to drift apart, solo efforts sapping investment in the group project. All the same, the album is magnificent and demonstrates just how good they had become a mere three years since their inception.

### **'The Thrill Of It All'** (Ferry)

Roxy had a knack for arresting opening tracks – 'Re-Make/Re-Model', 'Do The Strand', 'Street Life', as well as 'Manifesto' and 'More Than This' in later years. 'The Thrill Of It All' is up there with the very best – a dense roiling beast of a track that manages to stay compelling all the way through its six and a half minutes. Actually, it needs all that time to say its piece, as the edited version on *Greatest Hits* (1977) and the even shorter American single mix make clear.

The instrumental opening is all threat and foreboding, with the piano giving way to a simmering guitar solo and a massed chorus of Ferrys building the tension until the vocal melody takes off.

Well the sky is dark
The wind is cold
The night is young
Before it's old and grey
We will know the thrill of it all

While the lyrics are fairly banal, Ferry's phrasing makes them impossibly exciting. When he slips from 'young' to 'before' without pausing, it disrupts the scansion of the lyrics but uncovers new depths by allowing him to put all the verbal emphasis on 'grey'. It only gets better from there.

Your time has come
It's getting late
It's now or never
Don't hesitate or stall
When I call
Don't spoil the thrill of it all

Again, the phrasing carries it – the strategic pauses and then the rush to the half-rhyme he extracts from call/spoil, after which there's an instrumental break introduced by a buried saxophone figure. An entirely new melodic figure questions the adrenaline rush of the first verse: 'Before you go to sleep at night/Preying shadows/Do they ask you why?' with the haunting backing vocals 'Calling you, calling you'. And then the rush is back, Manzanera blazing, Jobson's strings conjuring the wind screaming over a blasted heath.

All the instruments are fighting for a place, mixed distinctly enough to parade their individual virtuosity if one strains consciously to isolate it. But collectively, they offer a wall of sound that's unlike anything else in the Roxy canon.

Even compared to the unholy caterwaul of 'Street Life', 'The Thrill Of It All' makes a truly monstrous racket. It is also very much a product of the studio. None of the live versions in circulation come close to capturing the power of the recording, which is perhaps the best evidence for John Punter's vital role in making *Country Life* as good as it is.

Three more verses, and it's hard to pick the most impressive lyrical acrobatics or the most arresting imagery:

Every word I use
Each crumpled page
Strange ideas
Mature with age
Like leaves when Autumn falls
Turn gold then they hit the ground

Every time I hear the latest sound
It's pure whisky
Reeling round and around my brain
Oh and all of that jive
It's driving me wild the dizzy spin I'm in

Try to decipher how much Ferry crams into just those lines. He manages to set the British English 'autumn' against the American English 'fall' while bringing back the primary meaning of the verb 'to fall' with reference to the leaves that cover the ground by the end of whatever one calls that particular season. Or take the pure whisky reeling, most obviously evoking the way a drunk reels across the road in the aftermath of too much liquid gold, but then also clearly referencing the circularity of the traditional Highland dance, not to mention a subtle recall of the previous verse, because good whisky – especially Highland whisky – does indeed mature with age. And surely he's also referencing the venerable advertising trope – then and now a staple of men's lifestyle magazines – that uses women, whisky, cigars and expensive cars as shorthand for success. By 1974, of course, the band had tasted both money and success, and Ferry was well set on the path to marrying into the gentry and defending his Eton-educated son's enthusiasm for fox hunting.

But he's also still smart enough to satirise his own ambition in song, even as he was becoming ever-more evasive, even hostile, in interviews. In the following lines, he remains ambivalent about the choices he's made: 'For all the pleasure that's surrounding you/Should compensate for all you're going through'. Yes, he's pleased to be dancing at Annabel's, and yes, he'll admit to voting Tory, and no, it doesn't make him entirely happy.

Then the roar picks up again, more wall-of-sound, and the sheer tenacity of the track really starts to tell. There are three more verses, all just as ripe for annotation as the rest, crowned by one of Ferry's most complicated vocal displays.

When you try too much
You lose control
Pressure rises
And so I'm told
Something's got to give
Oy vey!
High life ecstasy
You might as well live

Reduced to prose, it's not much of a lyric, but his embellishments are breathtaking. After 'something's got to give', Ferry's 'Oy vey!' – though patently ridiculous for an Englishman of his age and background – goes straight through into the strangulated 'Aaahh, high life ecstasy', his voice jumping from 'high' to 'life' and from 'ecs' to 'sta'. After that, he reverts to his normal voice with a 'You might as well live' that sounds like he's sellotaped that Dorothy Parker quote to his bathroom mirror. On its face, it's risible. On record, it's like a window into the soul of someone who knows he's forever given up on the place and the people he came from, someone who would do it again, even though it's tearing his sense of self to pieces. It's the quintessential illustration of Caroline Coon's insight into Ferry's dilemma (for which see the discussion of *Siren*) – what he wants and what he appeared to have achieved by 1974 is a betrayal of the class he was born into. Even worse, even if everyone else believes he's actually achieved his self-transformation, he knows, somewhere deep inside, that he will never be able to believe that he actually has.

'The Thrill Of It All' has Ferry's most fully realised vocal since 'Beauty Queen' – actorly in the best possible way. He's given meticulous thought to the way we derive linguistic meaning from the stresses we put on any given syllable. And there's more, of course – a final verse of contained hysteria ('I can't see/I can't speak' etc.) and an outro of fierce Manzanera guitar with Ferry's final words being a long cascading 'No, no, no, no'. But 'You might as well live' is the master key to mid-period Roxy. Amidst the lushest, baroque musicality they ever mustered, and the most verbally rich lyrics Ferry would ever write, there stands a man who is getting everything he ever wanted and is dying inside as he does it.

**'Three And Nine'** (Ferry, Mackay)

Andy Mackay's musical contribution to the Roxy sound is often underestimated, but he was there at the very beginning, and his oboe playing, in particular, was always one of the band's distinguishing features. 'Three And Nine' is one of the few pop songs in history built around an oboe part, with Ferry's vocal melody serving as a counterpoint to Mackay's woodwind. The lyrics, meanwhile, are both surprising and inspired.

It takes a perverse kind of genius to combine a treatise on the decimalization of British money with an ode to the grand movie palaces of the early 20th century. Gauzy nostalgia was part of Roxy's schtick from the very beginning. The name 'Roxy' conjures the Odeons, Rialtos, Apollos and, yes, Roxies of Ferry's youth. 'Do you remember how it used to be?/3 and 9 could show you any fantasy'. In the 1950s, three shillings ninepence was the price of a ticket into the cinematic world of Bogart, Gable and Astaire, on whose classic style Ferry had always modelled himself (see, for example, '2 H.B.' on *Roxy Music*). Here, he takes us from 'parti-coloured pictures' to 'B-feature back rows', assuring us that all this is 'No cheap nostalgia conjured up by me'. But in love and in the movies, as in currency, there's 'No point pretending/Change is here to stay'. In this new 'decimal romance', apparently, 'If you've warmed to centigrade/You stand a sporting chance'. It's not the kind of lyric that translates well to print, where the conceit falls a bit flat. But over the woozy oboe, plus Jobson's violin, every word makes sense in the way absurdity often does. Ferry's vision is nostalgic, but he's right to say it isn't cheap. He's fully aware that the technicolour universe he's celebrating existed amidst the black-and-white conformity of the 1950s, which the 1970s – with Roxy very much to the fore – were proud of having escaped.

**'All I Want Is You'** (Ferry)

The only UK single on the album (the US got an unsympathetically edited version of 'The Thrill Of it All' instead) reached a slightly disappointing number 12 and never became a highlight of the live set. But it's a perfect example of why John Punter was so good for the band.

The track opens with a noisy guitar intro that barely keeps the feedback in check before the rest of the instruments crash in behind one of the Ferry-most of Ferry openings:

Somebody told me just the other day
That you're leaving me, we're through
But if you knew how it hurt me so
Then you'd change your mind, I'm sure

It's the thrown away 'I'm sure' that clinches it: so confident in its lack of confidence. The music is straight-ahead driving rock, devoid of subtlety but absolutely packed with instrumental detail. As Ferry's opening salvo makes clear, there's a directness and literalism to the lyrics, which do without the rich allusions of the best Roxy tracks. 'Don't want to learn about etiquette/From glossy magazines/Why should I try to talk correct/Like they do in other scenes?'. It's still clever, though, the way he rhymes etiquette with correct in a grammatically incorrect fashion. But does he really mean it when he says, 'Don't want to know about one-night stands/Cut-price souvenirs'? After all, the one-night stand is one of the signature Ferry themes. Against Manzanera's lashing solos and Mackay carrying the melody on heavily treated sax, Ferry gives us:

If you ever change your mind
I've a certain cure
An old refrain
It lingers on
*L'amour, toujours l'amour*

At one level, this *is* ridiculous. But Ferry knows it, and as a memorable *Top Of The Pops* performance showed, he had a total belief in his own lack of conviction.

**'Out Of The Blue'** (Ferry, Manzanera)

This is the album's long-term keeper, a staple of both Roxy and Ferry solo shows, and one can see why. As recorded, it's a rare showcase for Eddie

Jobson's strings and closes with a wigged-out electric violin solo. But Manzanera's arrangement is so versatile that other instruments have been substituted at various points in the song's live evolution, not least for an extended funk-bass and percussion workout on the *Manifesto* tour. Throughout, Mackay and Thompson are at their most supportive, letting Manzanera's perfectly judged guitar work dialogue with the vocals, especially on the fifth, emphatic verse, which occupies the space where you'd expect to find a chorus:

Out of the blue
Love came rushing in
Out of the sky came the sun
Out of left field came a lucky day
Out of the blue
No more pain

Between each of the three couplets, Manzanera lays down a different lick, all of them perfectly formed. Here and on the long coda, Manzanera finds himself in surprisingly complete sync with Jobson. As Manzanera told David Cavanagh in *Uncut* in 2009, 'Because of my fondness for Eno, I was like a stroppy teenager when Eddie joined ... but, in fact, he ended up becoming one of my best friends in the band'. Whether the friendship or the musical compatibility came first, 'Out Of The Blue' and 'The Thrill Of It All' are the first Roxy tracks on which Jobson's violin is integral to the sonic effect.

Also, the lyric here is Ferry at his least fussy. 'All your fears/I fear I once shared', 'Not so long ago/I was so scared', 'I don't mind/If it's only/A passing craze'. Like 'All I Want Is You', this is a song where straightforward declarative sentences take the place of allusion and misdirection. But in any of his lyrical modes, 'Throwaway lines/Often ring true' could pass for Ferry's philosophy.

**'If It Takes All Night'** (Ferry)
The closest the album comes to an actual throwaway is this walking blues, anchored by boogie-woogie piano and harmonica. 'Oh here it comes/That old ennui/I hope it won't stay long' is Ferry flirting with self-parody, but knowingly so, and the entire performance feels like a sly wink at the listener. 'I'm only searching for the truth/And I'll find it if it takes all night' is palpably insincere, while 'If music be my mistress/Then at least she's Madame Claude' is darker than it seems. Between 1961 and 1976, Fernande Grudet – known as Madame Claude – ran the world's most famously exclusive prostitution network, among whose rumoured clients were John F. Kennedy and Gianni Agnelli, not to mention the whole of France's political elite. Were one to take the lyric seriously, then Ferry's mistress – his muse, if you will – turns out to be for sale and not for him alone, and it's hard to say whether he's implicating just himself here or the entire world of popular music. Either way, he undercuts any potential seriousness with a jaunty '*d'accord*' before

Mackay's sax solo. Finally, Ferry deploys his rare knack for nailing the delivery on the histrionic last verse.

Ah! More champagne
To lose this pain
Would be very nice
So I'll help myself to one more drink
And I'll find myself
If it takes all night

It's all a ruse, of course. He's already found himself, and sometimes – as 'The Thrill Of It All' lets us know – he doesn't particularly like what he's found. 'If It Takes All Night' seems to be arguing that selling your soul for success has a funny side, too. He would know, so perhaps he's right.

**'Bitter-Sweet'** (Ferry/Mackay)

Closing the A-side with a barroom piano flourish worked perfectly. Beginning side two with a slice of Weimar *noir* is inspired, all camp promise of fun to come. The contrast is best appreciated on vinyl, where you have to pause and turn the record over – the two songs' stylistic juxtaposition is stark enough to be jarring on CD or streaming. 'Bitter-Sweet' is this album's song for Europe. In a characteristic piece of one-upmanship, the band channel the spirit of Bertolt Brecht and Kurt Weill rather than just covering their 'Alabama Song'. Astonishingly, Roxy manage to transcend pastiche, forging a credible homage. How? It opens with tubular bells, followed by bass, and then a discordant blast shatters the hush. Horror-movie piano plinks in the background as Ferry pulls out his *Sprechgesang*: 'Well this is such/A sad affair'.

The song's dynamic contrasts are deliberately (and effectively) disconcerting, from brushed percussion and hushed whisper ('Every salted tear/It wrings/Bittersweet applause') to stomping cabaret threat ('High-stepping chorus lines mean I'm forgetting'). Add to that a rejection of verse/chorus/bridge structure in favour of extreme dynamic contrasts between quiet and loud verses, the loud ones all oompah rhythm and dissonant guitar slashes. In the second set of slow verses, 'How rich/In contrast love can be/Sometimes I'm quite amused/To see it twist and turn/To taste both sweet and dry' is just a setup for 'These vintage years/Lovers you consume, my friend/As others their wine': prime Ferry wordplay. 'These vintage years' is mere *cliché*, but it recalls the sweet and dry of the previous line and the 'more champagne' of 'It Takes All Night', which both stand in contrast to the earlier 'salted tears'. Then, the second of the loud cabaret passages is delivered entirely in German, which Ferry mauls even more painfully than he does his French. It translates as 'No, this is not the end of the world/Stranded between love and art' – which proves that while everything about 'Bitter-Sweet' and indeed *Country Life* is over the top, the band know it and they like it like that.

**'Triptych'** (Ferry)

The most neglected track on the album, and surely the worst, 'Triptych' suffers from two real defects. First, while Roxy almost always avoid pretentiousness by winking at the audience and deflating themselves, here, their virtuosity preens itself just a little bit too much. The song has a three-part instrumental structure. Instruments, lyrics and choir evoke a Renaissance altarpiece, Golgotha on one side, resurrection on the other, and the crucifixion itself at the triptych's centre. And second, as with 'Psalm' on the previous album, there's something slightly queasy about the religious content. You're forced to ask, is he serious? Is he doing detached irony? Is he poking fun? Is he just showing off? Put another way, the track's real virtues are also its main vices. The musical detail is very impressive. Keyboards pose as harpsichords, the triptych's framing panels are paced like Gregorian chants, while the central panel erupts into gigantic Vaughan Williams-style harmonies with at least four Ferrys in multi-tracked chorus.

'Triptych' is the sound of a band doing a thing simply because they were capable of doing it. They do it very well, but you can see why people don't love it.

**'Casanova'** (Ferry)

The *Country Life* track that contemporary reviewers of the album cited for its excellence was this one. With the decade headed towards its mid-point and all the cool kids having moved on from glam, it became clear that the genre's thuggish side was going to outlast its clever and artier one. Nowadays indulged as 'junk-shop glam', this long tail of bandwagon jumpers and no-hopers chased one another to the cutout bins while Sweet and Slade devolved into parody or tried to break America. Having helped found the glam aesthetic before walking away, Roxy took a look at the present state of what they'd wrought, gave it a shake, and asked the obvious question: what would this shit sound like if it was actually good? And they brought it. A murky mid-tempo funk rhythm straight out of Sly Stone's *There's A Riot Goin' On*, wah-wah effect behind Manzanera's guitar flourishes, while Mackay interjects nasty, sour sax lines between verses.

This is music that perfectly matches the lacerating lyric:

You the hero
So many times
You've loved
And didn't linger

That's a nicely succinct summary of the Casanova myth, but then:

Now my finger points at you
Another loser

Ferry makes the internal rhyme of 'linger'/'finger' sinister, and the way he enunciates 'loser' is positively venomous. Given how Ferry played at Casanova himself, it's hard to avoid the impression that he's talking about himself here:

You an island
On your own
Complete
In every detail
Monumental
A precious jewel
Or just a fool

He's 'courting more despair', there's 'no hope, not a glimmer' now that he's 'flirting with heroin, or is it cocaine?'. In fact, Roxy's druggy years were yet to come, and *Flesh + Blood* (1980), in particular, was to suffer from a surfeit of the white powder. But there's prescience here, an awareness that Ferry's path to the good life was stalked by bad vibes.

That's only clear if you listen closely to the lyric. If you don't, what you hear is a stomping piece of hard rock, pumping its fist and throbbing with barely contained aggression. There's a reason *Country Life* was the first Roxy album to crack the US top 40 (albeit barely). You could imagine 'Casanova' on FM radio sandwiched between Bad Company and Kiss, but it wasn't released as a single, and American programmers were flummoxed by the edit of 'The Thrill Of It All'. Still, 'Casanova' remains one of the key tracks of Roxy's middle period, and its quality as a composition is made clear by how well it survived the disco-fication Ferry inflicted on it in his solo version.

### **'A Really Good Time'** (Ferry)

'You're well educated/With no common sense'. By the standards of 1970s gender politics and male-dominated songwriting, it's a fairly mild rebuke. The wistfully pastoral music – opening with lulling sax and carried throughout by piano – is a perfect and deliberately incongruous backdrop to an otherwise stereotypical portrait of a woman living too fast.

All your troubles come from yourself
Nobody hurts you
They don't care
Just as long as you show them a really good time

Yes, Ferry's lyric is gendered, but if you switched every 'she' to 'he', the song would still make sense, which is another argument in mitigation.

All the things you used to do
A trip to the movies

A drink or two
They don't satisfy you
They don't tell you anything new

In verses like that, he could be talking to himself. Jobson's string-section orchestration is the musical star here, sweeping the melody along, carrying the piece from one verse to the next. Ferry's delivery is pitch-perfect, breezy ('You know I don't talk much/Except to myself'), and then forceful ('Listen to me/I'm not finished yet'). However ambivalent one feels about its sentiment and attitude, it's a lovely little track and a reminder that – as he confessed on 'Mother Of Pearl' – Ferry has always had a weakness for a simple tune.

**'Prairie Rose'** (Ferry, Manzanera)
This final track is an oddity. It contains all the pieces that make 'The Thrill Of It All' almost perfect, but some core element seems to be missing. A sighed, sibilant 'Texas' precedes Ferry's slide into his classic croon: 'Oh, that's where I belong, it seems to me'. Do you really, Bryan? And why? But, of course, Ferry's play-acting and some of the other lines here are actually quite good ('I will compose in fancy rhyme/Or just plain prose'). Unfortunately, his knack for phrasing deserts him. His singing is always mannered, but here, the mannerisms are unhealthily exaggerated – the offbeat pauses, those audible intakes of breath in syntactically unnatural spots, the unnecessary octave jump from 'I'd better leave right away' to 'I can hear you calling me'. Every one of these vocal tricks has worked for him in the past because they've helped to convey meaning – perhaps he's pausing for thought, perhaps it's indecision that's jumbled up his syntax, or maybe that sudden yelp is supposed to signal love-lorn desperation. In isolation, or when more carefully deployed, Ferry's vocal tricks signify. Here, jammed into just one track, they're reduced to tics.

And the instrumental backing – for all its undoubted virtuosity – can't rescue Ferry from himself. Thompson's good judgment remains unerring, and Mackay's sax freakout reminds us of his love/hate relationship with old-time rock 'n' roll. Manzanera knows when to provide structure, when to pull shapes, and when to drop a massive vulgar dose of guitar heroics into the mix. Three years earlier, when they first combined these disparate approaches, it was their *naïveté* that had made it so thrilling. Now, their transparently consummate skill on a series of sequential solos feels like slumming.

The contrast with the bridge on 'Grey Lagoons' on *For Your Pleasure* – which this track resembles structurally – is especially telling. Unlike the anarchic amateurism of its predecessor, every component of 'Prairie Rose' proclaims its technical excellence, while the song itself never quite gels. That said, in a funny case of life imitating art, Ferry was to fall for young Texan supermodel Jerry Hall shortly after the release of *Country Life*. He spent

**Above:** Early promotional photo of the band in the clothes that appear on the inner gatefold of *For Your Pleasure*. Clockwise from bottom left: Brian Eno, Phil Manzanera, Bryan Ferry, Paul Thompson, Andy Mackay. (*Alamy*)

**Above:** Gatefold sleeve art for *Roxy Music*, starring Kari-Ann Moller. (*Island/Reprise*)

**Above:** Inner gatefold art for *Roxy Music*. Clockwise from top left: Phil Manzanera, Andy Mackay, Bryan Ferry, Graham Simpson, Paul Thompson and Brian Eno. (*Island/Reprise*)

**Above:** Gatefold sleeve art for *For Your Pleasure*, starring Amanda Lear, Bryan Ferry and a black panther on a lead. (*Island/Warner*)

**Above:** Inner gatefold art for *For Your Pleasure* with Brian Eno, Phil Manzanera, Bryan Ferry, Andy Mackay and Paul Thompson. Note the absence of the album's bassist, 'guest artiste' John Porter. (*Island/Warner*)

**Above:** The band at the Crystal Palace Garden Party, London, on 19 July 1972, during Rik Kenton's brief tenure. (*Alamy*)

**Below:** Playback in the control room at Command Studios, Piccadilly, London, during the *Roxy Music* recording sessions in 1972. (*Getty*)

**Above:** Roxy performing 'In Every Dream Home A Heartache' on *The Old Grey Whistle Test*, first broadcast on 3 April 1973. (*Rex*)

**Below:** Roxy at the Royal College of Art on 5 July 1972. Left to right: Brian Eno, Phil Manzanera, Rik Kenton, Bryan Ferry, Andy Mackay and Paul Thompson. (*Brian Cooke*)

**Above:** Gatefold sleeve art for *Stranded*, starring Marilyn Coles. (*Island/Atco*)

**Above:** Inner gatefold art for *Stranded* with Phil Manzanera, Andy Mackay, new recruit Eddie Jobson, Paul Thompson and Bryan Ferry. (*Island/Atco*)

**Right:** Sleeve art for *Country Life*, starring Constanze Karoli and Eveline Grünwald. (*Island/Atco*)

**Left:** Sleeve art for *Siren*, starring Jerry Hall. (*Island/Atco*)

**This page:** Stills from the performance of 'All I Want Is You' on the Dutch music program *TopPop* on 1 December 1974.

**This page:** Stills of the band miming to 'Love Is The Drug' on ITV's short-lived *Supersonic* program on 11 November 1975, with backing singers The Sirens, Doreen Chanter and Jacquie Sullivan.

**Right:** Sleeve art for *Viva!*, starring Ferry and The Sirens. (*Island/Atco*)

**Left:** Sleeve art for *Manifesto*, starring mannequins posed by Anthony Price. (*Polydor/Atco*)

**Right:** Sleeve art for *Flesh + Blood*, starring Aimee Stephenson, Shelley Mann and Ashley Bolton. (*Polydor/Atco*)

**Left:** Sleeve art for *Avalon*, starring Lucy Helmore. (*Polydor/Warner*)

**Above:** Promo shot for *TopPop*, December 1973. Left to right: Eddie Jobson, Phil Manzanera, Bryan Ferry, Paul Thompson, touring bassist Sal Maida, and Andy Mackay. (*Gijsbert Hanekroot*)

**Below:** At the Holiday Inn, Manchester, October 1973. Left to right: Eddie Jobson, Phil Manzanera, Andy Mackay, Bryan Ferry, Paul Thompson and touring bassist Sal Maida. (*Jorgen Angel/Redferns*)

**Right:** Bryan Ferry with touring bassist Gary Tibbs, live on German TV in 1980. (*David Redferns/Redferns*)

**Left:** A still from German music program *Na Aowas!* on the *Avalon* tour, 26 April 1982, with Andy Newmark on drums and Alan Spenner on bass. (*Alamy*)

**This page:** Stills from the performance of 'More Than This' on German music program *Na Sowas!* on 26 April 1982.

**This page:** Stills from the official promo video for 'Avalon', filmed at Mentmore Towers, Bucks., with the three remaining core Roxy members, Ferry, Manzanera and Mackay, in 1982.

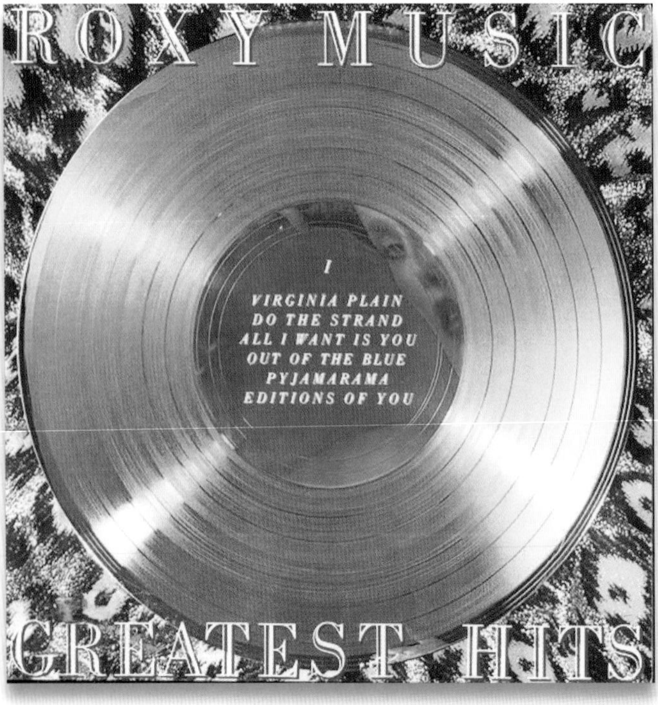


**Left:** Sleeve art for Roxy's *Greatest Hits*, 1977. (*Island/Atco*)

**Right:** Sleeve art for *The Thrill Of It All* four-CD compilation, 1995. (*Virgin*)

much of 1975 and 1976 explaining the strange allure of his new prairie rose to the press, only to have her leave him for Mick Jagger. Perhaps, as the song suggested, he should've left right away.

**Related Material**
**'All I Want Is You'** b/w **'Your Application's Failed' (single)**
Personnel: as above
UK release date: October 1974
US release date: not released
Charts: UK: 12, USA: -
Running time: 2:53/4:46

**'All I Want Is You'**
This is the album version, though it's worth noting that a 7" single at 45 RPM increases the song's wall-of-sound noisiness for the better.

**'Your Application's Failed'** (Thompson)
This was Paul Thompson's turn (his only one, in fact) to get a writing credit, and it's another instrumental B-side. Thompson wrote it whilst fiddling around on guitar and brought it into the studio, where the others helped to work up an arrangement. It has a nice swing and is lightweight in the manner of Manzanera's 'Hula Kula' on the B-side of 'Street Life'. Over louche bass and syncopated drums, Mackay steps in with a striding Stax-style sax solo, and then we get Manzanera guitar blasts along with some toy-town keyboards from Jobson. Then, they all come in at once in the familiar Roxy Mk II fashion. There is a series of guitar-punctuated drum fills, halfway through which Thompson exclaims the song title in an almost implausibly broad Geordie accent. Apparently, the words are those with which he was turned down for a job with the London Underground. Sax to the fore – except during an Eno-esque organ solo – everyone then revs things up for the final minute.

Of all the Roxy B-sides, this is far and away the most fun, but no one has ever said whether Ferry was anywhere near the studio when it was recorded.

## **Siren** (1975)

Personnel:
Bryan Ferry: voice, keyboards
Andrew Mackay: oboe, saxophone
Paul Thompson: drums
Phil Manzanera: guitar
Edwin Jobson: strings, synthesizer, keyboards
John Gustafson: bass
Produced by Chris Thomas
UK release date: October 1975
US release date: November 1975
Charts: UK: 4, USA: 50
Running time: 42:30

*Siren* is a good album, but not a great one. It lacks the edge of previous Roxy albums and is much less adventurous even than *Country Life*, which was already more conventional than its three predecessors. But taken on its own terms, *Siren* is a modestly experimental, song-oriented piece of mainstream 1970s rock. Many fans and critics saw that development as a betrayal. Many did and do concede that the album backs away from what Roxy's early incarnation promised. In a 1977 discussion with Ian MacDonald in the *NME*, Brian Eno maintained that the band should have quit after *Stranded* (ostensibly and magnanimously his favourite Roxy album), leaving an immaculate legacy: 'If the band had broken up then, it would've been sensational. It would've been one of the great phenomena. The other two albums rather let it down'. Fair enough, you think, but also not quite right. Roxy never stopped evolving; it's just that *Siren* was an evolution towards the middle of the road, and that was and is ideologically offensive to fans of Roxy Mk I. Where *Country Life* still held echoes of Eno-era Roxy, nothing of that was left on *Siren*. The Roxy Mk III that debuted in 1979 was something else again, but you can see why *Siren* was the end of the line for Roxy Mk II. There's nothing new this lineup could've said.

Less audibly, though obvious after the event, by 1975 the band were getting thoroughly sick of each other, as people will when forced to live in one another's pockets for too long. The year had opened with another North American tour – not as disastrous as previous ones, but hardly a success outside unlikely pockets of fandom in Cleveland and Detroit. From there, they'd proceeded to Japan and Australia, where the sheer distances between shows ensured that frayed nerves stayed frayed. Still, Roxy were not the sort of people for punch-ups or public blowouts – just a bit of peevish sniping in the press that fueled the speculation already aroused by the penumbra of solo Roxy projects (Mackay's *In Search Of Eddie Riff*, Ferry's *Another Time, Another Place*, Manzanera's *Diamond Head*) and various extracurricular activities with Eno and others. Everything was exacerbated by the breathless coverage of Ferry's social life and his succession of paramours threatening to overshadow discussion of the music. His most recent muse was 19-year-old Jerry Hall – a Texan model he'd seen on the cover of *Vogue* and immediately become obsessed with. She would be the star of Roxy's most famous record cover.

In mid-summer 1975, in the hitherto friendly *Melody Maker*, Caroline Coon published a quietly devastating portrait of Ferry that, in its 4,000 words, contained more insight than anything else published about him during Roxy's first five years. Its central analysis is worth quoting at length because it has never been bettered:

> (Ferry) has come a long way since he left Co. Durham in 1968. Leaving his working-class background far behind, he has been on a self-confessed quest for refinement and finesse. That he should remove himself so far from his roots – there is hardly a trace of a Northern accent when he speaks – is worth examining. There are basically two breeds of rock 'n' roll musicians. Some are working class and have exploited their inarticulate but expressive origins to the full with an uncompromising punk image and sound, like Family, Status Quo and Ian Hunter. And there are the educated middle-class musicians like the early Soft Machine, Pink Floyd, Yes and Mick Jagger, who, while using the medium of rock 'n' roll, have always had the freedom to augment their music with references from their highly articulate heritage. Ferry falls between the two. He is not middle class, but he is educated. His music speaks to that sensitive raw nerve of insecurity in anyone who is trying to move out of one class, which is a betrayal, and into another, which is to risk being an outcast. A new generation of upwardly mobile, educated working-class fans can easily identify with his torments and aspirations.

Then her analysis turns vicious:

> He aspires to a cultural style which is the antithesis of Newcastle's bleak Victorian back streets. But so far his attempts at finesse and refinement have been as rustic as Rousseau's attempts to paint realistically were primitive. Which is not to say they have lacked charm ... The cover of *Another Time, Another Place* is the closest he's come to disaster. It misses the listless, aristocratic *Last Year At Marienbad* touch by a mile. José By The Pool Last Summer At Benidorm is more like it.

She goes on to illustrate – using Ferry's own words – just how miserable his quest for perfection makes him, how he would prefer to be a 'completely unknown figure' like Howard Hughes, and how he's 'always dissatisfied with everything'. She notes that he's always responding with an 'It's all so terribly boring' because (her words) 'it's the method Bryan uses to avoid admitting how very seriously he takes life'. Her conclusion is no cheerier:

> He still needs a constant barrage of media feedback in order to find his own style in other people's ready-made images. And since his heroes are images, which stare out at him, emotionless and inanimate – he sets himself impossible standards. Were his heroes flesh and blood, perhaps he would allow himself some human failings. As it is, he tortures himself with what he considers to be his imperfections.

Given Ferry's generally fractious relationship with the press in these years, it's remarkable to see how much candour Coon was able to coax out of her interviewee. One suspects that his overweening desire to join the gentry into which Coon had been born (her father was a Kent landowner, and she was a boarder at the ultra-posh Legat School of Russian Ballet from the age of five) induced him to lower his guard, in which case the glee with which she takes her scalpel to him feels a bit shabby. Certainly, Ferry was never this unscripted in an interview again, not even in his most bitter moments following the commercial failure of *The Bride Stripped Bare*.

*Siren* was recorded hastily in the late summer of 1975. The cover – another magnificent Anthony Price production – presents Jerry Hall as a predatory mermaid, in blue body paint and fins, smiling carnivorously from a desolate rock. Despite the wintry sea-blue tones against which Hall's siren disports herself, the photo shoot – on the island of Anglesey off North Wales – took place in blazing hot weather that melted all Hall's body paint into her pores and forced her to make the train journey back to London soaking wet and wrapped in blue-stained towels. The tale no doubt grew rapidly taller in the telling, but it doesn't sound like it was much fun for anyone. Still, the result was an enduring icon of the golden age of album sleeve art.

Critics had long joked about Roxy's sleeves crediting more people for the cover art than for the music on the records, as if that were somehow an aesthetic crime. With *Siren* – and for the first time – the joke hits home because the cover is indeed more adventurous than the music, which tends towards the conventional. 'Love Is The Drug' was an astonishing single but uncharacteristic of an album that leans heavily on mid-tempo numbers, with the expected lyrics of love and loss less obliquely formulated than before. It sounds fantastic, though. Mixes as dense as those on *Country Life* would have overwhelmed many of the compositions on *Siren*. Instead of the previous album's John Porter, Roxy brought back the reliable Chris Thomas as producer – a veteran of *For Your Pleasure* and *Stranded*, he gave *Siren* the instrumental clarity and open sound stage of the latter album. Yet *Siren* has a less organic feel than either of those albums, and there is a more obvious technological edge to the acoustics and a clinical, studio-bound quality to the vibe. It would be uncharitable to claim that the sound was consciously tailored to an American FM-radio audience, but it scored very nicely with that demographic and ensured that Roxy's end-of-year tour in the States was their most successful by some distance.

The setlists for the European and American tours that took the band from 1975 to 1976 tell their own story. Several audio documents survive from those shows, though they are mainly unlistenable audience recordings. But the 27 January Stockholm performance (bootlegged in Europe as *Why Do You Think I'm A Funky Chick?* and in Australia as *Silk Circles*) has acceptable sound quality and a representative setlist. The touring band was stripped down to just Ferry, Mackay, Manzanera, Thompson and Jobson, with Rick Wills on bass, but there were no dancers, no backing singers and no elaborate staging. The playing is instrumentally precise, the timing flawless, and Ferry is in fine vocal form on everything but the opener 'Sentimental Fool', where his off-pitch falsetto makes your teeth hurt. There are six songs from *Siren*, three from *Country Life* and two from *Stranded*. Roxy Mk I is represented by 'Sea Breezes', 'Virginia Plain' and a fantastically arranged medley of 'Re-Make/Re-Model', 'Do The Strand' and 'Editions Of You', the latter sandwiched between the two halves of 'Do The Strand'. But – and it's a big but – we get one solo workout from Manzanera on 'Diamond Head', one from Mackay on 'Wild Weekend', and – so we all know who's boss – Ferry gets two, 'The 'In' Crowd' and a closing 'A Hard Rain's A-Gonna Fall'. It's a wonderful performance; everyone's in top form, but there's no mistaking the fact that this is a group of people who have lost interest in their collective endeavour. The tour finished in the States at the end of March 1976, and unbeknownst to the public, so did Roxy Mk II. Past their critical prime, the band were nonetheless at the height of their commercial fortunes. No one called it a breakup, and no one came right out and admitted that Roxy were through. A live album – painstakingly assembled by Manzanera from three different shows across three years – sold well and included only those tracks that the four core members could agree on.

Jobson went on to work with American musician Frank Zappa and prog rockers U.K. and would not again share a stage with Ferry until their icy reunion at the Rock and Roll Hall of Fame. Manzanera got into production, a revived Quiet Sun, and another collective project, 801, which featured Eno prominently in its first incarnation. Mackay scored a massive and lucrative success with his soundtrack for Thames TV's *Rock Follies*, then travelled in China and based his solo instrumental album *Resolving Contradictions* (1978) on that experience. Ferry released a four-song EP in the UK that formed the core of the American compilation LP *Let's Stick Together* (1976); this added single B-sides dating back three years and was eventually released in the UK after selling large quantities on import. He then made two solo albums – the dire *In Your Mind* (1977), with its rote song-writing and anonymous FM-radio sheen, and the poignant *The Bride Stripped Bare* (1978) – and moved to L.A., where he sank into the lush indolence of Beverly Hills. He and Jerry Hall remained staples of the gossip rags, although at this point, the UK music press had largely written Ferry off as a has-been.

But America – where critics like Robert Christgau and Lester Bangs had long been resistant to what Roxy Music had to offer – was finally beginning to warm to the band. In 1976, *Rolling Stone* magazine (which set the mainstream critical pace in the States until the mid-1990s) released the first edition of its *Illustrated History Of Rock And Roll*, with articles by the cream of the contemporary music press. A lush, oversized folio with 400 pages of text and scores of exclusive full-page photos, it was a genuinely groundbreaking attempt to explain the evolution of popular music from Elvis up to the date of publication. Like its parent magazine it was entirely American in outlook, but it also tried to do right by pop and rock in the other Anglophone territories. Along with the expected takes on The Beatles, The Rolling Stones, The Kinks, The Who and Led Zeppelin, there was an estimable contribution on art rock and glam (David Bowie, Lou Reed, Mott the Hoople) and a concluding chapter on 'The Shape Of The Seventies' written by editor Jim Miller. The five artists/music scenes he chose to illustrate the sound of the moment were Steely Dan, Disco, Reggae, Bruce Springsteen and Roxy Music. So it happened that Roxy's most laudatory stateside evaluation to date appeared when the group itself had ceased to exist: no small irony. But the praise was high indeed: 'To fashion albums filled with relatively straight love songs that come out sounding like a version of the Decline of the West is no mean feat … Torch songs from the crypt ... Ferry oscillates unpredictably between camp and deadly seriousness – and when Roxy gets serious, they can be scary, even repugnant'. Ferry's 'compulsive hedonist is doomed to a life of ephemeral satisfactions', but it is 'precisely this reduction of affection to the level of a narcotic that makes Roxy's music evocative of decadence and which gives the band's persona its cutting edge'.

Whatever one thinks of *Siren* in retrospect – good as it is, it remains a mixed bag – it broke the band in America and gave them permanent status there as niche 'quality artists' – less than superstars but more than cult favourites. After *Viva!*, the international fan base was kept satiated with an expertly compiled *Greatest Hits* (1977) that ignored chronology, skipped one single, and included four key album tracks. It was out of print by the end of the decade and never issued on CD; since superseded by newer but inferior compilations, it is still the finest summary of Roxy's first five years.

No one would've been surprised had the Roxy story ended with *Siren*, but neither was anyone shocked when, in 1979, they emerged from their hiatus. By leaving the scene when they did, they'd effortlessly avoided damnation during the punk wars, and just before the turn of the decade, they returned to a public ready to hear them again with fresh ears.

### **'Love Is The Drug'** (Ferry, Mackay)

Footsteps crunching on a gravel drive – 14 long paces in all. We're in the leafy stockbroker belt, not pebble-dash suburbia. A car door shuts with a satisfying thunk, a six-cylinder engine revs, the bass starts to throb, and Mackay hits us with the sax riff that carries the song. Ferry's lyric is brutally simple, his flash

Lothario trolling for whatever the singles bar has to offer: 'Love is the drug/ And I need to score'.

Thompson's drums and Gustafson's funk bass carry the sparse instrumentation, which acts out the urgent, pulsating hunger of having been 'spare for days'. The chord changes alone might've assured the band a hit, but Chris Thomas put everyone through their paces. As Mackay explained to David Chiu in *The Quietus* in 2015, Thomas forced him to do dozens of takes till he'd honed the sax riffs to perfection. Manzanera's contribution is mostly decorative embroidery in service of the propulsive rhythm. This most famous of Ferry's lyrics came out fully formed. Mackay: 'Bryan pulled one of his alchemical stunts and sang an almost complete vocal line with fantastic lyrics, to general amazement and applause in AIR Studio No. 1 late one night'. This was a particular achievement because Ferry often tinkered obsessively with lyrics till the very last minute. And you can see why his colleagues were impressed: 'Face to face/Toe to toe/Heart to heart/As we hit the floor' is very exciting. 'The locked embrace/The stumble 'round/I say go/She say yes/ Dim the lights/You can guess the rest'. The whole lyric pivots on that final genius line, which winks knowingly at the listener while also deflating the entire premiss of the song. However compulsive the desire, Ferry seems to be saying, however *necessary* sexual release might be, too often it's nothing more than that, a momentary respite from some greater need. The hooky chorus of 'oh oh' might sound celebratory, but this song is about sex without love against a backdrop of disco balls, velvet and leatherette.

It's incredibly catchy, enough to have reached number two in the UK, and it gave the band their first top-30 entry in the States. Nowadays, it's the only Roxy song one's likely to hear on the radio, and it's been an obligatory fixture in live sets for almost five decades. It's impossible not to dance to, but there's a cruelty in its heart that's a bit too explicit for comfort.

### **'End Of The Line'** (Ferry)

This is an exceptionally pretty song that succeeds on the basis of a lilting country swing, Jobson's plangent violin and Thompson's unerring instinct for when to show off. After three consecutive albums of Ferry indulging his talent for wordplay, here he begins to experiment with the pared-back simplicity he would eventually perfect on *Avalon*. 'Think I'll walk out in the rain', he begins, and the song's whole first half sighs by on a languid current of melancholy. Ferry pulls off precisely one lyrical surprise in the second verse – 'Reached the point of no return/The more I see, the more I stand alone': after the first verse's rhymed couplets, the ear is again primed for a rhyme (perhaps 'stand to learn') that it doesn't get. Until the lyric was published decades later, it was easier to hear 'stand to lose' than 'stand alone'. But either way, the wording upsets expectations nicely.

After a Jobson/Manzanera instrumental section, the vocals return with Thompson's descending drum fills, emphasising Ferry's now more declarative delivery. He's coasting lyrically with the likes of 'Now's the time to take a dive/Try a magic carpet ride', but the acrobatic way he bends 'ride' across five notes salvages it. Elsewhere, the forlorn lover act feels a bit rote:

Were you ever lonely
Mystified and blue?
Realising only
Your number's up, you're through

All told, it's as unchallenging a track as the band ever released and an unchallenging Roxy disappoints.

**'Sentimental Fool'** (Ferry, Mackay)
Where 'End Of The Line' finished on a long, slow instrumental outro, 'Sentimental Fool' opens with a long, slow instrumental intro, Mackay throwing sinister shapes over a creepy-crawly electric piano figure. Like some relic of the first album, this is a song of three separate parts, stitched together from early drafts of several songs and each highly distinct. The instrumental opening builds tension expertly, layering sound on sound quite deliberately until Ferry swoons in with a 'Surely you cannot be leading me on?' at the uppermost edge of his falsetto. 'Well if that's so/Oh never again will I love'. One wonders how many takes this first verse required in the studio, because he mangled it consistently in concert, unable to stay in key at that high an end of his vocal range. The lyric is not notably more complex or offbeat than on 'The End of the Line', which precedes it, but the strangulated vocal makes it feel much less conventional. 'How could I believe again?/How can I hold on?' Ferry cries, and then there's a key change, and we're off and away into a whole new song.

Sentimental fool
Knowing fate is cruel
You ought to forget it

Yes I know it's true
I've seen what love can do
But I don't regret it

And so it goes, three six-line verses, each a dialogue between the sentimental fool in love and a sensible admonitory voice inside his head.

Oh you silly thing
Can't you see what's happening?
You're better without it

No that's not the case
If you were in my place
Then you wouldn't doubt it

Sentimental fool
Who broke the golden rule?
You couldn't resist it

Though it's all in vain
I'd do it all again
Just to re-live one minute

The dialectical effect is achieved by a slight but detectable rebalancing of the stereo channels – the left channel for the cautioner and the right channel for the sentimental fool. It's a sonic trick that lends weight to Ferry's sharp but conventional words, and if it was Chris Thomas' idea, that alone ought to have earned him his production fee.

The song's third and final passage lowers the dynamic again, reverting to a minor key. The bright and ultimately optimistic tone of the previous part is replaced by a driving, almost motorik rhythmic churn as the lover's joyous infatuation becomes an obsessive need for a love that must go on and can't stop. But stop it does, on a false ending, succeeded by a quick snare fill, coda and another snare fill. The overall impact is expert and impressive, though it's constructed so clinically that one almost resents finding it so compelling.

**'Whirlwind'** (Ferry, Manzanera)
Not so this next, very likeable track. It's peak Manzanera and as close as Ferry comes on *Siren* to the torrents of wordplay that decked out the album's predecessors. The guitar comes crashing in over huge drum boasts and blares of guitar noise and Ferry howls:

Mayday!!
Cut down to size again
What then
When less is more, my friend?
All change
And let me start again

Straight-ahead hard rock, there's little useful to be said about 'Whirlwind'. The instrumentation throughout evokes the force of roaring waves breaking on the shore or the ferocious pressure of hurricane winds. You're carried away by the musical rush, which supports a jumble of Ferry imagery that you catch in tidbits of lyric here and there:

There she blows
Tear me down tornado
Whirlpool
Drag me to the deeps below

'Whirlwind/Crack your cheeks and blow', 'Earthquake/Shake me to my feet again', 'This case is closed/Elementary my dear'. All of them are rather good couplets, in their way, and 'Will a wildcat strike me tame?' is both incongruous as an image and also quite appropriate for the 1970s Britain of miners' strikes and three-day working week. Taken as a whole, the lyric doesn't cohere and certainly can't bear a great deal of analysis, but it's all very entertaining while it lasts and Manzanera's solo at the halfway point is among his most memorable. That said, it's a sign of a band running out of collective inspiration, everyone doing their part without creating something greater than their parts' sum. There's nothing wrong here; it's actually pretty good, but it somehow feels a bit ordinary.

**'She Sells'** (Ferry, Jobson)
Opening side two, Eddie Jobson's sole co-write on a Roxy album, has pace and tempo changes, rollicking piano and a shift into a darker mood at the end that's similar to 'Sentimental Fool'. Whereas the careful sequencing of other Roxy albums really does benefit from having to flip the vinyl disc over at the halfway mark, here the continuous play of a CD or streaming works perfectly well going from 'Whirlwind' to 'She Sells', which in turn tells you something about the homogeneity of *Siren*.

Some of Roxy's most compelling songs ('Virginia Plain', 'Pyjamarama', 'Grey Lagoons') sound meaningful thanks to Ferry's delivery, but make no literal, and very little figurative sense except as a collage of imagery. By contrast, on this track Ferry essays lyrics that sound like they want to mean something, even that they *should* mean something, and also clearly don't. 'I watch you walking in waltz time/A jigsaw puzzle in tune', 'Now you're fixing to fly me/Autoerotic pleas'. Not only do these mean nothing, they don't really evoke anything either.

Compared to the virtuoso metaphors with which Ferry describes his 'Mother of Pearl' on *Stranded*, here, his object of desire never really takes shape in the mind's eye. The one exception can be found in a single couplet: 'Made-up eyes/Make up my mind' is a devastatingly effective shorthand for the kind of romantic decisions that are made suddenly on the dance floor or while ordering drinks at the singles bar – as if the lothario we met in 'Love is the Drug' has grown some self-awareness. But it doesn't cancel out the vagueness of the imagery elsewhere, and the whole fourth verse is, let us say, of its time: 'She sells country and modern/Ancient western song/Of oriental confusion/You so right, me so wrong' would have slipped by unnoticed in the 1970s, but the pidgin syntax of the last line locates it in a historical moment when the comedian Peter Sellers pretending to be Chinese was a mainstay of mainstream humour. It's a reminder that however timeless Roxy still often sounds, their records were made half a century ago, and fifty years is a long time. Also, and perhaps a sign of creative fatigue and the haste in which *Siren* was recorded, Ferry threw away one of his best lines on a track as indifferent as this one. 'Rather nouveau than never', he sings, and by 1975, he was in a position to know.

### **'Could It Happen To Me?'** (Ferry)

> Do you know what it means to me
> To delight in your company
> Could it happen to me?
>
> Do you know what I'm certain of
> I would to fall in love
> Could it happen to me?

How you feel about this song will depend on your tolerance for Ferry at the edge of self-parody: 'If a tear's a crime, then I must confess', 'Let us sing of the tortured heart/And the lonely soul in this world apart', and plenty more where those came from. From one angle, it feels like a pleasing lightweight; from another, it's Ferry teetering over the abyss that found him (according to Allan Jones) proclaiming of a hotel in Cardiff that 'One looks at a room like this, and one rather thinks it looks like a council flat'. If that sounds as if he's in danger of taking his bored playboy schtick too far, it's because he is. When he sings, 'My old world charm isn't quite enough', it rings painfully true, just not in the way Ferry must've hoped it would. While there's no doubt that his relationship with the music press was uniformly toxic at this point, moments like this went out of his way to provoke the attacks.

Musically, the song is quite charming, melancholic, slower passages alternating with jaunty verses. There's some very attractive sax work from Mackay, and Thompson is at his no-nonsense best, but they're not quite enough to compensate. There's an adolescent self-pity to the lyric, and Ferry was old enough to know better.

### **'Both Ends Burning'** (Ferry)

In 2015, Mackay told David Chiu that 'Both Ends Burning' was one of several tracks that got overworked as an instrumental before Ferry brought in his lyrics and that, as a consequence, it has always sounded better live. He's absolutely right. The final Roxy Mk II single could've been an absolute blinder, but it was burdened with a lot of sonic decoration that was simply unnecessary. The strange, conga percussion that chatters along in the intro is a good example of the problem, as is the syrupy synth that gums up the clarity of Manzanera's guitar and Mackay's sax, both of which are in particularly fine form.

The lyric is a comprehensive exploration of love-as-fire/fire-as-love tropes, as Ferry wonders how he'll survive the ardour that's burning inside. 'Will the fires meet/Somewhere deep in my soul tonight?'. Mackay's sax blows all over the melody, sometimes as prominent and as hooky as on 'Love Is The Drug'.

Having taken an age over the lyric, Ferry gives the singing his all, not just managing a soaring octave leap on 'Tell me will it never end/Put your foot around the bend' but carrying the last word across two beats before 'Drive me crazy to an early grave'. This is where he recovers his ability to make meaning reside in the phrasing and intonation. The whole thing fades out with a classic, flowing Manzanera solo that echoes the now-concluded vocal melody with extended virtuosity.

As a single, 'Both Ends Burning' fared poorly, the saturation coverage of Ferry's personal life and the rumours of dissension in the Roxy ranks taking their toll on sales. In truth, the over-elaboration of the studio version sapped the song of its inherent strength. But it had a powerful live presence, as the version on *Viva!* makes clear.

**'Nightingale'** (Ferry, Manzanera)

'Nightingale' really is a pleasing lightweight and another track that toughened up very nicely live. The nightingale is a staple reference in Western culture, from the mourning Penelope in Homer's *Odyssey* to 'A Nightingale Sang In Berkeley Square', which a young Ferry could not have escaped, whether in its Bing Crosby or its Vera Lynn incarnation. And we can be sure that Ferry's nightingale is a traditional literary topos and not a memory, because even before recent catastrophic population declines, nightingales never ranged north of the Humber.

Ferry approaches the lyrics like a writing assignment – draft eight stanzas exploring every possible way in which the archetypal singing bird can serve as a metaphor for love and loss. It's a gimmick he'd used before (mutability on 'Just Like You', hymnody on 'Psalm', sunset on 'Sunset', etc.) with good results.

Now when the moon is high
Shall we, nightingale
Duet all through the night
A pair of souls for sale?

Stars cluster, glistening
Captive till the dawn
Patiently listening
They've heard it all before

Innovative, no, but the craftsmanship is palpable. The vocals convey emotion through emphasis and elocution rather than unexpected phrasing, and the music elevates the entire exercise.

As he often does on his co-writes, Manzanera brings a brisk playfulness to the music, precisely where Ferry would go for the portentous. The guitarist is a famously agreeable figure in an industry not known for them, and instrumentally, 'Nightingale' is an ensemble piece, not a show-off showcase for his guitar-playing. That's clearest in the fine instrumental section – Mackay winds a sinuous oboe part around a shimmering Manzanera chord progression, while Jobson ratchets up tension with bursts of violin, and all three cut loose as Ferry returns:

Should I stay here, should I go?
I couldn't bear to be alone
Was it really love I saw?
Oh, now I'll never know

However close this incarnation of the band may have been to dissolution, when they all pulled towards a single goal as they did here, they demonstrated that music needn't be particularly novel or complex to still be gripping.

**'Just Another High'** (Ferry)

*Siren* opened with Ferry hooked on love as a drug. By the end, he's telling us that love's just a game one plays, just another high. Roxy's album closers rarely claim the attention of their stunning opening tracks, but they often deserve to, like here. As on 'Sentimental Fool', one detects the importance of *Siren*'s producer Chris Thomas and engineer Steve Nye. The soundscape is crystalline but airless, as if recorded in a bell jar. The instrumental and vocal separation is immaculate, with every note on every instrument individually articulated.

The speed is funereal, the melancholia terminal. Over Mackay's clavinet, Manzanera's opening chord progression creeps and jabs, the aural approximation of a vicious hangover. A bleary-eyed Ferry is too worn out to properly sing: 'Maybe your heart is breaking/I wouldn't know, now would I?'. The party is over, the guests have gone home, and all that's left is the detritus of too many things unsaid, other things spoken all too clearly: the aftermath of love, anaesthetized but still a misery. Thompson kicks up a disconcertingly jaunty rhythm as Ferry ruminates towards the chorus: 'I'm just another crazy guy/Playing at love was another high/Just another high'. Thompson – habitually sparing with cymbals and hi-hat – here generates most of the song's dramatic tension by punctuating the vocals with his crash cymbals.

Ferry carries the melody while keeping to his speak-singing mode till just before the instrumental section and gets in some deceptively simple lines: 'Marriages made in heaven/Can they survive in this life?' – where 'Can they survive' is easily heard as the equally effective 'Can be survived'. 'I really blew my cool/But you, you just blew out the candle' gets across on that repeated, redundant pronoun. 'Didn't you try just another high?/Didn't you sigh as you waved goodbye?'. A hanging pause, a breathless emphasis on the 'good' in 'goodbye', and Manzanera takes up a solo that echoes the melody's main motive. Mackay slides in with some sympathetic sax doubling, and Thompson announces a return of the chorus with a double-stroke roll and cymbals. The final verse starts meditatively but ends with a declaration:

Lately it seems so empty here
But I suppose I'm alright
Maybe tomorrow's not so clear
Still I remember that night
Singing to you like this is
My only way to reach you
And though I'm too proud to say it
Oh, how I long to see you

Just before 'singing to you', a female backup chorus picks up, enhancing while also mocking the sentiment and casting doubt on the apparent sincerity of the final chorus and its altered lyric:

Shattered my dreams by your goodbye
Scattered my hopes, they fill the sky
Desolate am I

It all ends with a two-minute postscript, as Ferry wonders if he should start anew and find someone who'll love him as much as he once loved his departed dream girl.

Nowhere in the track's six and a half minutes is the music less than tuneful; nowhere does it suggest a sense of threat, and yet it ends exhausted and desolate. On the first track of their first album, Roxy had been sure that the next time was the best time, and it felt like the truth. Five albums and just under four years later, there is no next time and starting anew isn't an option. That feels like the truth, too.

**Related Material**

**'Love Is The Drug'** b/w **'Sultanesque' (single)**

Personnel: as above
UK and US release dates: October 1975
Charts: UK: 2, USA: 30
Running time: 4:11/5:26

### 'Love Is The Drug'

Discussed above. This unrelenting single is identical to the album version.

### 'Sultanesque'

Roxy's worst B-side ever is a Ferry keyboard doodle with some half-hearted Manzanera guitar decoration, a drum unit and vibes from Jobson. That they let their famous quality-control slip so badly on this one is evidence of how little gas the band had left in their tank at this point. It's hard to imagine that anyone who bought this single for its A-side played the B-side all the way through, let alone more than once.

### 'Both Ends Burning' b/w 'For Your Pleasure (Live)' (single)

Personnel: as above
UK release date: December 1975.
US release date: not released
Charts: UK: 25, USA: -
Running time: 3:58/4:59

### 'Both Ends Burning'

The single version of this track is an edit of the album version, chopping eight bars off the intro and eight bars off Manzanera's extended solo at the end, shortening it by well over a minute. The edit does no real damage since it leaves the song's structure intact. But neither does it correct the issue of over-instrumentation discussed above.

### 'For Your Pleasure (Live)'

Pulled from an October 1975 show at the Empire Pool, Wembley, this is a relatively straight version of the original composition. As heard on bootlegs of the *Siren* tour, this performance would originally have segued into Manzanera's 'Diamond Head' in a truly inspired medley. A slow, meditative track from deep in the back catalogue is rather an inscrutable choice for a single B-side. Perhaps – as was the case with 'Sultanesque' – its release merely demonstrates that all concerned had, at that point, lost interest in Roxy. It certainly can't have helped the single's chart performance.

## Viva! (1976)

Personnel:
Bryan Ferry: voice, keyboards
Andrew Mackay: saxophone, oboe
Paul Thompson: drums
Phil Manzanera: guitar
Edwin Jobson: strings, synthesizer, keyboards
John Wetton, John Gustafson, Rick Wills, Sal Maida: bass
The Sirens: backing vocals
Produced by Chris Thomas
UK and US release date: July 1976
Charts: UK: 6, USA: 81
Running time: 46:15

When Roxy went on hiatus after *Siren* – its members immersed in their various solo and collaborative ventures – they were at their commercial peak, so it made sense for them to put out some new product. It's not clear whether the band or the label provided the impetus for the release of *Viva!*, but it made good business sense, and Roxy had never pretended they weren't interested in money. They here rediscovered their traditional approach to quality control and made some good artistic decisions. First – in that era of *Frampton Comes Alive* and Thin Lizzy's *Live And Dangerous* – they chose a single disc (albeit in another lovely gatefold) rather than a bloated live double. Second, they tasked Manzanera – their most diplomatic member – with making a first cut from hours of available live tape, after which they only included those songs – and those versions of songs – that all four core members could agree on. Third, instead of a single concert or even a single tour, they picked numbers from three venues, three tours and three different years, hence the four bassist credits (including Rick Wills, who was on Roxy's final tour but didn't actually appear on this album). Finally, with track selections made, the band turned to the ever-estimable Chris Thomas to weave a coherent vibe through the eight tracks they'd selected. Every one of those choices turned up trumps. Even the 1974 Newcastle City Hall concert (which is widely available as a bootleg) – in perfect professional audio and from which five of these eight tracks come – isn't first-rate from end to end. Likewise, performances of *Siren* tracks on the late 1975/early 1976 tour were of pretty variable quality, judging from the tapes in circulation, but 'Both Ends Burning' deserved better than its studio version, and this Wembley cut is a stormer.

*Viva!* thus succeeds on an artistic level, given that it is what it is (live product in *lieu* of foreseeable new material), and it did just fine commercially, too, reaching a respectable number six on the UK charts, and cracking the *Billboard* top 100 in the States. As a portrait of the band, it's partial at best, and the following year's *Greatest Hits* is more of an aesthetic triumph. But thanks in large part to Chris Thomas' sympathetic editing, *Viva!* feels like a complete and enjoyable album in its own right. The notes below merely indicate salient or interesting aspects of the live versions, without fresh comment on the songs *per se*.

**'Out Of The Blue'** (Ferry, Manzanera)
This is one of the album's five tracks from Newcastle City Hall, October 1974, with John Wetton on bass. The big surprise is Mackay's oboe lines at the beginning of the track, which are revealed as more important to establishing the song's melody than one would realize from the studio version. The rest of the arrangement is very similar, though Thompson keeps the rhythm going more relentlessly, and Jobson's electric violin is given particular prominence in the coda.

**'Pyjamarama'** (Ferry)
One of two tracks from the Glasgow Apollo on the *Stranded* tour, with Sal Maida on bass. This version of Roxy's second single slows down the guitar chords of the intro, giving Thompson more space for drama. Ferry's vocal, also somewhat slower, is delivered in his normal singing range rather than the falsetto of the studio version, which helps bring the melody more clearly into focus. Shorn of Eno's gadgetry, both Mackay's sax solo and Manzanera's guitar solo over the outro are rendered more conventional. Though 'conventional' is not usually a word of approbation when it comes to Roxy, this is a track that actually benefits from its transformation – the obtuseness and inaccessibility of the original make way for the very welcoming pop song that had been hiding inside.

**'The Bogus Man'** (Ferry)
From the Newcastle show, this runs for a mere seven minutes compared to the nine-minute studio version. But it's still almost twice as long as the arrangement Roxy pulled together in 2022 for their 50th-anniversary tour. Speeding the tempo up ever so slightly and adding some swagger to the vocal, it's neither better nor worse than the original. And it still goes on forever.

**'Chance Meeting'** (Ferry)
This second Glasgow Apollo track also takes an Eno-era number and shears away a lot of the craziness. Ferry's vastly more controlled vocal is a highlight, but one misses the sonic weirdness and alienating sound separation of the *Roxy Music* original, particularly the enormous distance between vocal and instrumental tracks in the mix. More troublingly, the fearsome guitar dissonance of Manzanera's original performance is completely gone, and with it goes everything that made the studio version more than a curio. The weakest track on *Viva!*.

**'Both Ends Burning'** (Ferry)
The sole track taken from the 1975 Wembley show with John Gustafson on bass, this is a truly vast improvement on the *Siren* original. Many critics hate the backing vocals from The Sirens (Doreen Chanter and Jacquie Sullivan), and it's true that they're not recorded or mixed particularly sympathetically, but they don't detract from the commanding power of Ferry's lead vocal. And even if they had done, stripping away all the studio trickery and aural wallpaper of the original transforms a song that felt sodden and lead-footed into a propulsive, rhythmically daring dance track. It's an anthem about doing everything for love and more, even if it burns you up and burns you out in the process.

Mackay's sax part is just as riveting speeded up, while the concision that the live format forces onto Manzanera's closing solo is also a huge asset. Had the single version of this track been delivered with the kind of force and drive we get here, it might've done a good deal better in the charts.

**'If There Is Something'** (Ferry)
The album's indisputable triumph, this is another Newcastle City Hall number. It's hugely extended from the studio version's six and a half minutes to nearly 11 without any of it sounding like prog indulgence. Instead, this brings out all the drama and contrast inherent in the original, with everything from Manzanera's guitar to Ferry's vocals vastly more confident and convincing.

The opening country-rock pastiche swings more naturally and Ferry doesn't essay his 'American' styling, adopting a straightforward and tuneful vocal that puts the lyric across without fuss. Jobson makes himself felt in the song's second part, his violin revealing his classical training, and Manzanera's transitional riff is serpentine and vaguely menacing. Ferry's over-the-top 'I would do anything for you' verse is delivered without the old crack and strain, which makes his 'Growing potatoes by the score' that much more surprising and effective. After which, things break into extended instrumental passages that never feel like muso chin-stroking. The original Manzanera guitar section is extended by a good half minute or more and then gives way to an extended Jobson solo on electric violin. Dropping the dynamic, Mackay gets some time with his original oboe part, subjecting it to some effects-pedal distortion. And then electric piano and drums slowly build the drama, syncopated piano punctuated by some of the most authoritative work Thompson ever did, live or in the studio. The whole choral coda is magnificent and celebratory, with Ferry in his finest vocal form, sounding as if he actually had a *good* voice, a tutored one. It's a pretty good song made great: no mean feat.

**'In Every Dream Home A Heartache'** (Ferry)
Also from Newcastle 1974 and also much extended from the studio original, this is an excellent performance, without being transformative. Ferry's vocal

is perhaps too theatrical and emphatic, which risks making the lyric sound comic rather than blankly threatening like it did in the studio. The ensemble playing is flawless, but all the places in which this improves on the original are down to Manzanera. In the early, slow, recitative verses – while Mackay keeps up the woozy underpinning – the guitarist pops declarative, nasty comments over Ferry's vocal. Then, when the whole song explodes after 'But you blew my mind', Manzanera goes berserk for a full three minutes, without Eno's trickery and without the strange fade to silence, in what is both a fine example of guitar heroism and an inspired send-up thereof.

**'Do The Strand'** (Ferry)
The fifth and final number from the Newcastle show, this is a pretty straight read of the studio version, which was beyond improvement anyway. Ferry's vocal is commanding, especially on the 'They're playing our tune' lines. And the way the band illustrate 'Tired of the tango' with a snatch of tango rhythm, 'Weary of the waltz' with a waltz, and so on, is as funny as they meant it to be. It's an appropriate and thoroughly enjoyable way to round out the album.

## Manifesto (1979)

Personnel:
Bryan Ferry: vocals, keyboards, harmonica
Phil Manzanera: guitar
Andy Mackay: oboe, saxophone
Gary Tibbs, Alan Spenner: bass
Paul Thompson: drums
Paul Carrack: piano
Produced by Roxy Music
UK and US release date: March 1979
Charts: UK: 7, USA: 23
Running time: 42:23

*Manifesto* is distinguished by being no one's favourite Roxy Music album. With *Flesh + Blood,* it's a fixture in the bargain bins of secondhand record shops. The distinctive disco-era sensibility of the cover art – mannequins clothed and posed as if conversing at a swish party – has not aged well. Only 'Dance Away' has won a lasting place in the live Roxy repertoire, though Ferry has occasionally unearthed other songs from the album for his solo tours. Nearly half the tracks on *Manifesto* are throwaways that feed the mood and the groove but are individually inconsequential. Surprisingly, two of the album's three singles – 'Trash' and 'Angel Eyes' – fall into that category, as does much of side two (called the West Side on the original vinyl), where 'Cry Cry Cry', 'My Little Girl' and 'Ain't That So' slip pleasantly by until the swooning 'Spin Me Round' dances us out on a high note.

At the time and ever since, no matter what denials Ferry and Co. have issued, *Manifesto* looks very much like a flight back to the safety of Roxy after the disappointment of Ferry's solo *In Your Mind* (1977) and *The Bride Stripped Bare* (1978). The former – an attempt to write straightforward rock songs with an eye on American success – is one of the weakest collections of Ferry's career, but the latter is excellent. Wounded by Jerry Hall's leaving him, Ferry had poured his heart into *Bride*, with four original compositions and six well-chosen covers. It remains to this day the least stylized and most sincere thing he's ever done. But its critical reception was mixed, and it tanked commercially, leaving Ferry – touchy at the best of times – defeated and at sea. Rounding up the old gang (minus an embittered Eddie Jobson) must've seemed like a good idea, and Phil, Andy and Paul come gamely through. Thompson, in particular, is in top form – the power, the solidity, and the total lack of fuss in his drumming are what stops the more flimsy tracks from floating away altogether. That he would be ejected before the recording of the follow-up album is – in retrospect – one of the worst artistic choices Ferry ever made. But *The Bride Stripped Bare* had given the singer a taste of working with top session wizards and he'd become enamoured of what could be woven from the tasteful virtuosity of the multitracks. *Flesh + Blood* was to take that formula to the bank, but *Manifesto* – thanks to Thompson – is a much better album. It's said that drummers Steve Ferrone and Rick Marotta played (uncredited) on some of the tracks here: while that has never been properly documented, there are a few drum parts that don't sound much like Thompson and the drummer did allude to Ferry's plan to work with Marotta in a 1995 Mojo interview with Rob Chapman. Alan Spenner's bass is forward in the mix without being obtrusive, and when he's at his most inventive (on 'Still Falls The Rain', 'Stronger Through The Years' and the astonishing title track), it marks real progress in the evolution of the Roxy sound.

Refreshed by solo work (Mackay's *Resolving Contradictions*, Manzanera's *Listen Now* and *K-Scope*) and Mackay's best-selling score for the Thames TV hit *Rock Follies*, the pair have more writing credits on *Manifesto* than on any other Roxy album. Yet almost none of the tracks feature the consecutive solo showcases that were such fixtures of Roxy Mks I and II – guitar, sax and keyboards are all subordinated to the service of the groove here. That's also true of Ferry's lyrics for the most part, which eschew the puns, puzzles and *jeux d'esprit* of his younger self, except where he gets serious: on 'Still Falls The Rain' and 'Manifesto' itself. But the vocals ride the rhythm and centre the vibe. *Manifesto* may well be Ferry's *best* vocal performance in the conventional sense until his brief early-21st-century renaissance. He's learned to control the vibrato now, turns his falsetto on for clear effect, and can finally handle the low end of his range without singing flat. He's also still enunciating – treating words as words rather than sound effects, as he began to do on *Avalon*.

On *Manifesto*, you can hear premonitions of Ferry's future blandness and Manzanera/Mackay's muzak-bound 1980s as The Explorers, but only if you look for them. Taken on its own terms, *Manifesto* is a very real success, and not just because it was Roxy's highest-charting album in the US. They had stopped out of the game during the punk era, instantly saving themselves from the contempt heaped on other early 1970s sensations, and instead becoming touchstones for many post-punk pioneers. Rather than coming back the same as before and risking accusations of working to a formula – or worse still, imitating their young progeny – they switched gears altogether. *Manifesto* is an ocean away from the Jobson trilogy and a whole universe away from the Eno albums, but it's also nothing like what the band became for *Avalon*. This was demonstrated on a gruelling world tour that began in Sweden in late February 1979, took in Germany, France and Holland, and moved on to American and Japanese dates before climaxing in May with three nights at London's Hammersmith Odeon. The *Manifesto* tracks transferred surprisingly well to live performance, revealing a sinewy, well-structured core, even in some of the throwaways – as best heard on the often-bootlegged Denver and Oakland shows, the former now available on an excellent, semi-official double CD called *Concerto*.

In the end, *Manifesto* stands by itself in the Roxy canon – an honourable experiment and a genuine attempt at moving on. It's no one's favourite Roxy album, but I've also never met anyone who hates it.

**'Manifesto'** (Ferry, Manzanera)

The first thing you hear on the first track of the first Roxy album since they went on hiatus for the first time (Roxy have never broken up) starts as it means to go on: with a sour discordant bass figure. Two and a half minutes of roiling instrumental follow, with Paul Thompson's mid-tempo thump underpinning all manner of dissonant strangeness from guitar, keyboards, and sax. But the real star is Alan Spenner's bass playing, which climbs spider-like up and down the instrument's strings. Given the clangour on top, it takes repeated listening to work out that it's the bass that's anchoring the surface *musique concrète* to the rhythmic rock foundation. Then, something starts to change. Chords begin forming under the racket, surfacing briefly, then going under again, until suddenly, at the two-and-a-half-minute mark, they resolve into a major key, and Ferry begins declaring his manifesto. That's pretty weird in itself. Was there ever a band that made more out of doubt, ennui and the sheer inability to believe in things than Roxy? A band less likely to produce a manifesto? But here they are, the music suddenly forthright and declarative:

I'm for a life around the corner
That takes you by surprise
That comes, leaves, all you need
And more beside

And there's more where that came from: 'I'm into friendship and plain sailing/Through frenzied ports o' call', 'I'm for the revolution's coming', 'Hold out when you're in doubt', 'When you find an answer/Bring it home to me'. If you didn't know it was Bryan Ferry, you'd be forgiven for thinking it was promotional literature for Est or some other 1970s cult of self-improvement. 'Now and then I've suffered imperfection/Studied marble flaws' comes as a relief: it is still the old ambivalent Ferry, after all.

In point of fact, the lyrics really aren't terribly consequential. Certainly, they don't stand up to the scrutiny of Roxy's other great openers like 'Street Life' or 'The Thrill Of It All'. And yet, this *is* another great Roxy opener because Ferry's vocal drive is equal to the demands placed on it by the instrumental prowess on display. The vocal is rich and earthy, with none of the melismatics of the early days. It's also pretty convincing, Ferry bringing some of the muscle he had put into the handful of original songs he wrote for *The Bride Stripped Bare* and making you believe he believes in something. That's quite an achievement for one of music's great play-actors.

**'Trash'** (Ferry, Manzanera)

Despite being chosen as the album's first single, 'Trash' is a pretty feeble entry in the Roxy canon. It was greeted with critical derision, peaked at a lowly 40 in the charts, and Ferry now acknowledges it as among his weakest lyrics: 'Teenage fever/Oh you've got it bad' and variations on 'Only 17, bet you know the trash I mean'. He even seems to suggest that the titular trash is turning tricks: 'Go to Plaza/Where's the trade?'. It's ugly, and it's not redeemed by the music, which has perhaps the most annoying guitar timbre Manzanera ever achieved – buzzing like a wasp caught in a tin. In fact, it's the only *Manifesto* track that couldn't be rescued by its live arrangement.

**'Angel Eyes'** (Ferry, Mackay)

This was the final single to be drawn from *Manifesto* and was a substantial hit, though not in the original mix, which was only to be found on initial pressings of the album. The album version opens with some convincingly rocking guitar chords, as Spenner and Thompson lock into a loping groove that sounds organic and analogue – more vintage Philadelphia International Records than contemporary disco. In between the verses, the harmony modulates, while Mackay plays with some highly varied and, at times, heavily treated solos. Not for the last time, you're reminded that he did his most consistently interesting saxophone work on this album, buried though it sometimes is in the mix.

The lyrics are – alas – piffle. 'Oh angel eyes/Let your love light shine on me' indeed. Ferry is quite capable of rescuing a dodgy lyric with an arresting vocal or some thoughtful phrasing, but he doesn't do it here. Fortunately, after the indefensible rubbish that is 'Trash', the instrumental interest of 'Angel Eyes' at least encourages you to persevere with the album – a good thing because the reward is the next two tracks: both excellent.

**'Still Falls The Rain'** (Ferry, Manzanera)

To my ears, this is the album's finest track and certainly one that Ferry believed in deeply. As he invariably told audiences on the 1979 tour, it's a song about schizophrenia. Whether it was inspired by something real or was simply a lyrical conceit, Ferry leans into it and creates overlapping narratives of Jekyll and Hyde on the one hand and a nightclub crawler on the other. In other words, it's the final entry in a trilogy that began with 'Ladytron', continued with 'The Bogus Man', and concludes here with a dose of 'Love Is The Drug' thrown in for good measure. As for the music, this may be Manzanera's finest composition on any Roxy album, beginning with the guitar figure that opens the track over Alan Spenner's elastic bassline.

Dear Hyde<br>
No more can I explain<br>
I've tried<br>
With words in vain<br>
They pass you by<br>
Like falling rain<br>
From perfect skies<br>
Still falls the rain<br>
Inside

The image of rain falling inside the mind – perturbing, disconcerting, throwing it into confusion – is well done, as is the misdirection. The speaker knows that the rain is falling inside the mind, but he dissociates it into an address to an external monster. The music is slow, plangent and melancholy, Ferry's vocal near the top of his range, his phrasing suggestive of uncertainty, all rising intonations in odd places – 'vain', 'explain', the first 'rain'.

As the last line fades, Manzanera switches into a snarling little guitar run, and the rhythm changes into a hustling dance number, Mackay laying sax over rumbling, samba-style percussion. Ferry pitches his voice lower: 'Hey brother, don't be square' and 'I'm your man/Got it made/You feed my fire/ You need my shade'. The exaggerated, slightly comical hepcat vocabulary doesn't disguise the sense of threat: the predator hunting on the dance floor.

Suddenly, those opening guitar lines chime out again, and we're back into the slow passage, Ferry again singing in his upper range:

You're here Hyde
Once more inspire
This strangely tied
Uncertain frame
So torn inside
Still falls the rain
Two minds, one vein
Still falls the rain
Inside

Ferry wrong-foots us with that additional couplet and its perfectly formulated 'Two minds, one vein'. Then we're back on the dance floor, this time with a vocal harmony, as the monster, who was meant to have been kept outside, takes over:

Hey doctor
Don't be scared
It's you and me
So where's my share?
I'm the man, move aside
Call me Mister
Just call me Hyde

The opening guitar figure returns, but this time, there's no relief, no answering passage from the doctor, but rather another menacing boogie:

Hey lover don't be shy
I'm a single-minded guy
Better watch me
Boy I'm rough

Half a man
Ain't strong enough

A fourth occurrence of the opening guitar, and the doctor is now long gone. The monster reiterates his first verse and then we move to Manzanera's best guitar solo since 'Mother Of Pearl', while Ferry sings wordlessly and the whole band create a dense cushion of noisy support. It's very reminiscent of Roxy Mk II and is probably the closest Roxy Mk III came to the kind of layered wall of sound so characteristic of the Jobson years. Why this deep cut was never dusted off for live performance after the *Manifesto* tour is a mystery, but it's a magnificent track all the same.

**'Stronger Through The Years'** (Ferry)
Another deep cut, abandoned after the *Manifesto* tour until a brief revival for Ferry's 2014 solo shows. Lyrically, it's not quite in the same league as 'Still Falls The Rain', but it's on par musically and actually quite challenging.

A dark, roiling affair, it begins with a slow Yamaha electric grand piano and a classic Manzanera riff. The arrangement takes the fullest advantage of the sonic atmospherics made possible by the state-of-the-art synthesizers. There are all sorts of haunting embellishments hiding in the mix, the better to capture the mood of Ferry's lyric:

Through the undercover hours
Bad and bleak
To be brief, too much sorrow
And the flesh is weak

Then the sound opens up, blossoming into a cinematic roar, and Ferry gives us the chorus, positively booming in its lugubrious sorrow:

No more feeling
No more tears
The river's wide enough
Flowing stronger through the years

That's about it for the lyric – there's one more verse and then a repeat of the chorus. Perhaps it's another Jerry Hall breakup song: Ferry won't cry anymore because there's no more feeling left, and there's no going back to where he was because the river between the two them is only flowing stronger, becoming more forbidding as time goes by.

In between the verses, there's an instrumental section that gives the piano and guitar some space for delicate interplay. After the second chorus, there's more atmospherics, a blazing Manzanera solo, a lot of Spenner at his trickiest, and the same kind of cyclical repetition that characterised the second half of 'For Your Pleasure'. It's difficult to pinpoint any trace of Mackay on this track, but everyone presumably contributed to the intricate soundscape of the arrangement. The instrumental end section was extended to a full five minutes live, with Manzanera putting on a particularly virtuosic show and synths vamping until Mackay came in on the oboe, at which point the band would imperceptibly shift tempo and segue directly into the introduction to 'Ladytron'.

**'Ain't That So'** (Ferry)

Side two of *Manifesto* is so much about flow and musical patterning that tracks become hard to discuss individually. Their personalities, insofar as they have them, exist within the tidal surges and ebbs of the whole side. As live versions demonstrate, some of them were detachable from that context to the point that they sound like songs in their own right. But on the album, they're much of a muchness.

'Ain't That So' has a certain rhythmic interest and some tricky time changes, but the lyric is more-or-less mush: 'Dynamite/Such sweet surprise/In southern heat/Or northern skies'. There's a propulsion to the groove, but the dated percussive guitar wah-wah effect doesn't distract from the basic four-on-the-floor rhythm that Thompson lays down. There are some effective piano and synth breaks, along with thoroughly anonymous Manzanera guitar, but what rescues this overly long track from its own blandness is Mackay's sax-playing. Muffled but interesting during the vocal passages, it comes into its own on the breaks, in a succession of solo turns, each one different from the next. It's some of his finest work.

**'My Little Girl'** (Ferry, Manzanera)

You can hear Manzanera enjoying himself, getting funky. He's been listening to samba, disco, and reggae, as the chopping off-beat guitar takes us into a harder-edged dance track than the smooth Philly-Soul stylings of 'Ain't That So'. Alan Spenner's bass playing is almost as inventive as on the title track, and the guitar lines Manzanera inserts into the vamping section are engaging enough. Mackay is less central to the track's ambience here but gives his tenor sax free rein over the outro. Unfortunately, the backing vocals on the chorus (which is just the song title sung over and over again) are reminiscent of solo Ferry over-egging the pudding, and the lyric lines are again fairly stodgy:

There's a small café
Where lovers take their time
It's good for rainy days
Too bad the weather's fine

Not bad scene-setting *per se*, but it evokes chipped Formica and stewed tea rather than *un petit verre* in Paris drizzle. One can't be sure if the bathos is intentional, and that's not good.

**'Dance Away'** (Ferry)

This is a *bona fide* classic, an obligatory part of every live show ever since, and also the first time Roxy scored a hit with a perfectly conventional pop song, one that hadn't so much as a trace of the experimental or *outré* to it. According to Manzanera, it's one of the few songs none of them wanted to play live on their two reunion tours, though they did so dutifully because the audience expected it. The arrangement they now play is the single version, which became a hit after being remixed in New York. This album version is actually more interesting, with Mackay and Thompson in particular locking into an organic, analogue disco sound that was sterilised by the radio-ready sheen of the single remix.

As with its clear predecessor, 'Love Is The Drug', this begins with very effective sound effects – a match flaring, the sizzle of tobacco catching, and the satisfied exhalation that follows that first magic puff. Every smoker and ex-smoker can identify with the sound and the feeling, and in an era when everyone smoked, the listener just knew that Ferry was gearing up for the romance and adventure of a night on the town. When Ferry's singles-bar beauty passes by 'Hand in hand with another guy', she may be 'dressed to kill', but it's you-know-who that's dying. The whole lyric is a retreat from the gimlet-eyed cynicism of its predecessor, Ferry pretending to feel the pain of a genuine love lost rather than shrugging at the grotty aftermath of the latest one-night stand.

Musically, it's verse/chorus/verse/chorus/bridge/verse/chorus, without the sort of innovation one got from earlier Roxy incarnations. Also, as on too much of *Manifesto*, Manzanera is all over the track but buried so deep in the mix that he fails to make the impression he should. It's undeniable that Ferry rung variations on both the theme and structure of 'Dance Away' throughout his solo career. (As Jeremy Allen put it none-too-kindly in *The Guardian*: 'He hit on a formula to write the same oleaginous ballad over and over again, to handsome remuneration. (Play 'Dance Away' and 'Slave To Love' back to back, and you'll see what I mean.)' This initial iteration is by some distance the best.

**'Cry, Cry, Cry'** (Ferry)

The song opens with a horn line that echoes the basic melody of 'My Little Girl' closely enough that it's almost a reprise, and the whole track passes by quickly enough in a similarly inconsequential fashion. Again, as in 'My Little Girl', the lyric is no more than a sketch. 'Let us pray the Lord have mercy/ On your mercenary mind' is made worse by the pairing and the placement of mercy/mercenary, a weak gesture towards the old Ferry cleverness. The rest of the track is, if anything, worse: 'I'm fading out your hologram/A phony toothpaste smile' is meaningless, meritless, and if it's trying to convey futurism, it fails. The backing chorus of 'Cry, cry, cry, cry, cry' sounds like it's borrowed from Ferry's solo cover of 'The Price Of Love', which is not intrinsically bad, but is decidedly incongruous. The drumming lacks Thompson's distinctive personality and Manzanera throws in some country rock lines that contrast with the generic Thom Bell dance vibe that surrounds them. Again, it's Mackay who rescues what can be rescued, this time with some tasty interjections that sound like prime Maceo Parker backing James Brown. In other words, like most of the West Side of *Manifesto*, it's eminently listenable, but look for meaning at your peril.

**'Spin Me Round'** (Ferry)
By contrast, this one is just plain gorgeous and a minor classic in the canon. It's cyclical and repetitive in the best way, and despite its relative length, it doesn't overstay its welcome. Lyrically and vocally, it's a rough draft for 'Avalon'. But here, the oh-so-very-tired-now-the-party's-over motif is articulated with greater verbal precision:

Now the ballroom's empty
Everybody I know
Has been and gone

He's a 'netherworld dancing toy'. 'Does it matter to me who turns the key?'

Now if life is for living
Then the way is clear
But I don't understand

Why the dream has ended
Yet I can't wake up
Lend a hand

Spin me round

It's bleak in a way *Avalon* never is, which makes it a halfway house between the hedonism and exhaustion of Ferry's lyrics on *Stranded*, *Country Life* and *Siren* and the sighing embrace of the transient and ephemeral on *Avalon* and its solo successors.

The music here is delicate, synth to the fore, with discreet Mackay underpinning, and drums that this time *do* sound like Thompson – delicate snare and cymbals edging the bass and piano forward with some rather more demonstrative fills punctuating the final circling refrain of 'Spin me round'. It's hardly the sort of track one seeks out for its own sake, but it goes a long way towards redeeming the lyrical deficiencies elsewhere, making it the perfect conclusion to the side and really to the album as a whole. If it starts with a forthright manifesto, it ends, appropriately, with Bryan just 'a shadow, echoing on'.

**Related Material**

**'Trash'** b/w **'Trash 2' (single)**

Personnel: as above
UK release date: February 1979
US release date: not released
Charts: UK: 40, USA: -
Running time: 2:14/3:12

**'Trash'** (Ferry, Manzanera)
Identical to the album track and no more rewarding at 45 RPM than it is at 33, this was Roxy's lowest-charting UK single, a fate it thoroughly deserved.

**'Trash 2'** (Ferry, Manzanera)
This was a re-recording, slowed down, with a longer instrumental introduction before the main melody starts and the vocals come in. All it serves to demonstrate is that slowing down a bad, fast song gets you a slow song that's just as bad.

**'Dance Away'** b/w **'Cry Cry Cry' (single)**

Personnel: as above
UK and US release date: April 1979
Charts: UK: 2, USA: 44
Running time: 3:50/2:56

**'Dance Away'** (Ferry)
The single version of 'Dance Away' is a fairly radical remix of the album version, which it replaced on the second and subsequent pressings of *Manifesto*. It is less organic sounding than the original, with a more prominent drum unit pushing the dance rhythm forward. Ferry's voice is further forward in the mix, the transitions between verses are shortened slightly, and the long percussive break before the final verse is omitted. Manzanera is still sadly lost in the mix, but Mackay's sax sounds more emphatic beneath the final chorus and the backing vocals, very much of their time, stand out more prominently in this version. This is the arrangement the band have followed live ever since. While it's less aurally interesting than the album original (which is restored on the 2022 vinyl reissue), the single version is undoubtedly more commercial. It sounds like the hit it was.

**'Cry Cry Cry'** (Ferry)
Identical to the album version.

**'Angel Eyes'** b/w **'My Little Girl'**

Personnel: as above
UK and US release date: August 1979

Charts: UK: 4, USA: 23
Running time: 3:00/3:18

**'Angel Eyes'** (Ferry, Mackay)
As with 'Dance Away', the original album version was quite different from the version that became a hit (number four), and the single version replaced the original from the album's third pressing onwards. The single is a partial re-recording, done in an explicitly disco style, with more aggressive drums. Ferry's voice is isolated in the mix and given a distinct echoing sheen. The third of the original's four verses is cut, streamlining the arrangement while also giving Manzanera's ringing guitar embellishments more presence in the mix. The song itself is among Roxy's weakest (there's no salvaging these lyrics), but it was one of the best-selling singles of 1979 and featured throughout the *Manifesto* tour.

**'My Little Girl'** (Ferry, Manzanera)
Identical to the album version.

## Flesh + Blood (1980)

Personnel:
Bryan Ferry: voice, keyboards
Neil Hubbard, Phil Manzanera: guitar
Andy Mackay: saxophone
Alan Schwartzberg, Andy Newmark, Simon Phillips: drums
Alan Spenner, Neil Jason, Gary Tibbs: bass
Paul Carrack: keyboards
Produced by Roxy Music
UK and US release date: May 1980
Charts: UK: 1, USA: 35
Running time: 41:56

After the conclusion of the long *Manifesto* tour, the band dispersed for the remainder of 1979. Ferry made a TV appearance in a French soap opera as a lightly disguised version of himself; Mackay wrote an excellent book on *Electronic Music*, while Manzanera began work on what would become one of his best solo albums, *Primitive Guitars* (1982).

Early in the new year, the band convened at Manzanera's Gallery Studio to record what became *Flesh + Blood*. The band's first indisputable American success, *Flesh + Blood* holds an odd position in the Roxy canon. On the one hand, it features Ferry's most consistent singing on any Roxy album. He's still articulating every syllable; his falsetto is as bright and piercing as on the early albums, but now with his pitch under control, and he saves his trademark vibrato for special moments. But on the other hand, there's the lyrics and music. There's a lot of slippage here. It's not just the dismissal of Paul Thompson, whose old-school sense of rock rhythm had anchored even the out-and-out disco tracks on the previous album, but the overwhelming sensation of too much tinkering on tracks that didn't merit that level of attention. *Flesh + Blood* is the sound of money being flushed down the studio toilet. It's the sound of Ferry's tuxedos and sports cars come to life.

At times, Manzanera and Mackay function like two of the many session players in the room. Six years earlier, Mackay's sax sounded like no one else in the business. Here, he's allowed to cut loose only on 'Same Old Scene', 'Over You' and 'Running Wild'. Manzanera's contributions are hard to distinguish from those of ace session player Neil Hubbard, who was at this point halfway through his decade-long tenure as a Ferry sideman. And the lyrics? 'My Only Love' – an inexplicably permanent fixture in both Roxy and solo Ferry setlists – and the title track were to forever mark the nadir of Ferry's composing skills. And yet, the band included several songs from the album in the set for their 50th-anniversary tour. (On the American leg, 'Same Old Scene' was even substituted for 'Virginia Plain', both good songs, to be sure, but only one of them is historic.)

Ferry's sleeve concept for *Flesh + Blood* reverted to the cover girl themes of old. Three sculpted Aryan goddesses in white frocks pose athletically with javelins against a golden background. But just like the music, the cover image takes the daring of early Roxy and polishes the edge off it. Still, in 1980 there was no arguing with the album's commercial success. If *Manifesto* now sounds more artistically inspired, critics at the time were considerably more positive about this follow-up, and all three of its UK singles performed very well.

The European tour that accompanied the album ran from May to late July, recommencing early the following year, during which time *Flesh + Blood* had remained continuously in the album chart. It's a bit of a surprise that they didn't take the tour to North America, where Roxy sold more and more as they became less interesting. American critic Robert Christgau – who'd consistently misunderstood Roxy over the years – got it right for a change with *Flesh + Blood*: 'The secondhand funk is getting too easy to take ... and I always get suspicious when covers overwhelm originals'.

**'In The Midnight Hour'** (Pickett, Cropper)

The weakest track ever to open a Roxy album, this feels like one of the readymades Ferry has always dropped into his solo outings when short on inspiration. The brightness of the mix marks it out as Roxy of this vintage – it sounds shiny and expensive, with perfect separation between the instruments and lots of sonic space around them, Ferry's creamy drawl idling over sprightly backing. This is what Ferry must've wanted when he sacked Paul Thompson – Alan Schwartzberg's loping syncopated rhythm is more technically accomplished but vastly more anonymous than Thompson's playing could ever have been. There's no point in playing a game of 'Is it Manzanera or Neil Hubbard?' because both of them are on the track and the guitars are merely functional. Touring bassist Gary Tibbs makes his sole studio appearance with the band here, and the best one can say of Mackay's tenor sax-playing is that it offers a nice accentual counterpoint to the familiar melody. And familiarity is very much the problem. It's a lazy choice of song, one covered over the years by everyone from Bruce Springsteen to The Jam to The Grateful Dead. Ferry's an inveterate interpreter of other people's compositions, but that works best when he grabs a song in both hands and beats it up. When he just runs an arrangement through the Ferry-iser, it's at best pleasant and at worst fairly dull. This one's fairly dull.

**'Oh Yeah'** (Ferry)

This is a classic weepy – there's no denying that, even if you want to. Often, I want to. That it's a compelling composition is not something any sane person would try to deny. Your ears prick up at the interrogative piano chords, Manzanera's guitar in perfect counterpoint, each note hanging suspended in its sonic space.

The lyric, about falling in love to the sounds of the car stereo, is nothing special. There's an unidiomatic awkwardness to 'Driving you home from a movie show' – people just don't say 'movie show' – and that phrase recurs in every verse. But the chorus is aurally sublime. 'There's a band playing on the radio/To the rhythm of rhyming guitars', sung by harmonising Ferrys, his voice forthright and confident, while Manzanera enacts the rhyming guitar.

There's nothing novel here, nothing terribly clever. But the sentiments are universal – love won and lost – and the words really nail how important place and sound are to the way we process intense emotion. Plus, it's all very beautiful. That said, had Air Supply covered 'Oh Yeah', no one would've been surprised, which tells you what you need to know, for better and for worse.

**'Same Old Scene'** (Ferry)

It's an odd one, this. It's probably the most convincingly funky of all Roxy Mk III songs, and it's certainly their most musically interesting late-period single. The jittery percussion is top-notch, and Ferry's falsetto on the chorus is unusually effective. Manzanera is given a little bit of room to groove, there's a very catchy synth part, and Mackay plays a blinder of a solo over the outro.

The lyric is fairly pedestrian: 'Nothing lasts forever/Of that I'm sure', 'Young loving may be so extreme/Will I still survive the same old scene?'. But the second verse is a refreshing recollection of more interesting times:

> In our lighter moments, precious few
> It's all that heavy weather we're going through
> When I turn the corner
> I can't believe
> It's still that same old movie
> That's haunting me

Ferry wrings a lot of emotion out of his phrasing of 'precious few', and the juxtaposition of 'lighter moments' with 'heavy weather' is evocative and lyrical without needing to make literal sense. The familiar analogy comparing life to a movie is well deployed and somewhat barbed, as if Ferry's admitting that we've seen this film before.

There's a lot of footage out there of the band miming 'Same Old Scene' on various TV shows. The most striking example is from December 1980 on the Spanish variety show *Aplauso*, in which a gobsmacked Madrileño studio audience are staring wide-eyed as they watch a video of the band mugging for the cameras – Ferry in lime green, Manzanera in pink pastel, and Mackay in louche blue satin shirt unbuttoned halfway down his chest. Mackay, in particular, looks like he can't be bothered and even mimes what's audibly a synthesizer solo on his sax. One gets the sense that – seven months on from the album's release and many dozens of live shows later – the band were getting sick of their new repertoire. It's a shame to see it happen with 'Same

Old Scene', which is definitely among the album's best tracks, not least in comparison with what comes next.

**'Flesh And Blood'** (Ferry)

> My friend's flesh and blood
> She lies overtime
> You'd nail her if you could
> But she says 'Love me for my mind'

Just how much cocaine does it take to write that stanza and think it passes muster? This is the same kind of Ferry-on-autopilot that ruined 'Trash' on *Manifesto* – it's not only sexist, it's actually misogynist, and to make matters worse, it's just plain lazy, a sketch not a painting. One might argue that the lyric is of its time – that the masculine desire for sex, objectifying a woman who wants to be acknowledged as a real, thinking person, reflects an all too commonplace reality. Perhaps true, but there's none of the old Ferry ambiguity here, no subtlety to his 'So rude, she's no good/But as she says, it pays to win'. Add the portentous echoed chords that open proceedings (Ferry's first guitar-playing on any Roxy song), and *voilà!* – the worst song Roxy ever recorded.

**'My Only Love'** (Ferry)
The dire title track is followed by this, the *second* worst song Roxy ever recorded. The minor-key piano figure at the beginning only hints at the schmaltz that's coming. 'There's a river flowing/By the willow tree'. Compare, if you will, 'Boo-hoo willows weep around you still/Mirrored reflections of dew' from *Stranded*. One is poetic, nuanced, surprising, the other just trots out the willow as shorthand for sorrow. We also get unredeemed cliché: 'Does it seem so funny/For a fool to cry?'.

The longevity of this song is inexplicable. It's been in every Roxy tour and every Ferry solo show, year-in, year-out. Only 'Editions Of You' is similarly eternal, the difference being that it deserves to be. Truly, the only excuse for this song is that, in a live setting, it functions the way drum solos did back in the 1970s: Manzanera, Chris Spedding or whichever jobbing guitarist Ferry happens to have along gets a chance to cut loose while the maestro rests his voice.

Melodically, it bears a striking resemblance to the superior 'This Island Earth' from Ferry's *The Bride Stripped Bare* (1978). But whereas on that number, Ferry attacks the lyric with real gusto and powerful phrasing, here, he's content to slide into the sighing croon that would neuter most of his solo output from *Boys And Girls* (1985) right through to *Mamouna* (1994).

**'Over You'** (Ferry, Manzanera)
A great choice for the first single, this is a bit of pop fluff that's such fun you forgive how slight it is. One also forgives its sonic resemblance to

contemporary hit makers The Cars, who'd long been accused of ripping off Roxy.

All the excitement lies in the synth line, since Ferry's lyric is just his standard-issue lost-love fare:

Oh baby
How can I go on?
Crying so long
Over you
Where strangers
Look for new love
I'm so lost in love
Over you

Manzanera is surprisingly subdued, with just one dramatic chord setting up the final verse. Over the pillowy synth ending, Mackay plays one of the very best sax solos of his career. Unlike the blazing up-tempo squall he kicks up on 'Same Old Scene', here he's lyrical, injecting a melancholy, perhaps even a tragic note, that Ferry's lyric suggests without supplying. After a good minute of Mackay, the synth starts to dominate, the outro morphs into a slower, almost raga-like rhythm, and eventually cross-fades into the next track.

**'Eight Miles High'** (Clark, Crosby, McGuinn)
Unlike 'In the Midnight Hour', this is a very fine cover version and an unexpected one at that. Manzanera doesn't have the technical chops of Roger McGuinn, but he brings exotic, vaguely-Indian chromatics to a prominent guitar part that completely transforms the druggy folk of The Byrds. In place of the acid vibe of the 1960s original, you get the 1980s cocaine edition. Ferry sings like he's on day three without sleep, up there flying, above it all, observing every detail with the surreal detachment that comes with strung-out exhaustion. It's a performance, of course, and a knowing one, but it's lived in.

As with most of the album, 'Eight Miles High' doesn't reward extensive analysis, but given Roxy's long-standing attention to surface over depth, it's a convincing merger of form and function. The long ending is excellent and rhythmically audacious, and the chorus of Ferrys chanting the title over the outro really does sound as if they're about to float off into space, never to return.

**'Rain Rain Rain'** (Ferry)
That title should be warning enough. The mix is dense, the music thick and sticky, like trying to walk through tar. The synth flourishes are meant to punctuate the bass-heavy melody, but they're mixed too high and just sound unpleasant. To be charitable, that might be the point.

The lyric is boy-meets-girl, boy-meets-drugs, drugs win: 'Gonna last forever getting high'. It's nearly as sexist as 'Flesh And Blood', nearly as maudlin as 'My Only Love', and it kills the momentum of 'Eight Miles High' stone-dead.

**'No Strange Delight'** (Ferry, Manzanera)

The running time of this Manzanera co-write is 4:45, but it feels longer. More than any other track on the album, it anticipates *Avalon*. Though it lacks that album's airiness, the soundscape is nonetheless given more thought than the song here.

The vocal melody is a little bit too close to that of 'My Only Love', and the sonic density recalls 'Stronger Through The Years' on *Manifesto* without the epic grandiosity of that track's vocal. There's also a fairly satisfying reminiscence of the long, slowly decomposing fade-out of the classic 'For Your Pleasure'.

The lyric is a sort of cut-and-paste Ferry-by-numbers: 'Your poor heart skips a beat/Tearing back the years/To when you really cared', 'Now a slave to obsession/Your strange delight'. It makes more sense than some of the others on this album, but without inducing you to care. It's unfortunate, really, because all the pieces of a decent Roxy composition are here, yet some of them are stacked on top of one another, others are in the wrong place, and you've heard every one of them before. Although it is possible to derive a lot of pleasure from a familiar formula – even when you recognize it as a formula – that's only true if you get the ratio of ingredients right, which here, Roxy don't.

**'Running Wild'** (Ferry, Manzanera)

If there is a hidden gem or a lost cut in the Roxy catalogue, this is it, buried at the end of a disappointing album after two patience-trying dirges. 'Running Wild' deserves much better because it's a blindingly good piece of work, with every single player at the top of their game. A descending guitar figure intersects with a piano, the whole effect ineffably sad:

There's that melody again
Burning through my head
It does me in
Turns me right around
To my old friend
I wonder how you've changed

Yes, the theme is familiar: wondering what's become of a long-lost lover, turning the might-have-beens over and over in your head. But all Ferry's vocal nous is on display here. Though he was only 35, he manages to put a lifetime's sorrow into his performance, as he reaches for the first harmonised chorus:

Are you still
Running wild, like you do
When all your dreams come true?

The guitar and piano are still rolling gently, setting the pace, while the rhythm section is subdued and meditative going into the second verse:

Happy days you pretend
That your love will never end
There's that melody again
Where it's coming from
I must have been
Drifting out of time, now I'm in
Underneath you'll find
I'm just the same

The guitar becomes more emphatic as the chorus repeats, but this time it's about:

Running wild, like you do
When all your dreams fall through

But, Ferry reassures himself:

I could always pretend
That I'll fall in love again

At that point Mackay launches into his best moment on the album – an aching saxophone solo that echoes the vocal melody of the verses with almost impossible pathos. Under the last four notes of the solo, the piano walks back in, and Ferry returns to a third and final chorus:

Running wild, like you do
If only dreams came true
I could even pretend
That I'll fall in love again

Manzanera ascends into the most lyrical solo of his career, which, like Mackay's earlier one, is an echo of the melody. Manzanera soars while his and Neil Hubbard's rhythm-guitar parts interlock and spar with the lead, Ferry harmonising with himself on repeated cries of 'Running wild again'. With a flash of his old gift for phrasing, Ferry sings 'again' twice on the penultimate refrain to foreshadow the ending, after which Manzanera's solo spirals into its final chord.

Never performed live, never included on a compilation, but perfectly formed and beautifully recorded, 'Running Wild' is a triumph. One can't quite say it redeems the entire album, but the case could be made.

**Related Material**
**'Over You'** b/w **'Manifesto' (single)**
Personnel: as above
UK release date: May 1980
US release date: September 1980
Charts: UK: 5, USA: 80
Running time: 3:27/4:03

**'Over You'** (Ferry/Manzanera)
This is identical to the album version, with a fade-out rather than the album's segue into 'Eight Miles High'.

**'Manifesto'** (Ferry, Manzanera)
This is a re-recorded and completely rearranged version, unreleased in the US, where the 'Over You' single was burdened with 'My Only Love' as a B-side.

Whereas the brilliant album track was a wall of instrumental sound that gave way, after almost three minutes, to a continuous tumble of verses wihout a chorus, here Roxy attempt to transform 'Manifesto' into a conventional song. It was an interesting choice and an unlikely one. Remade with a synth-driven, disco rhythm, Manzanera's treated guitar carries the instrumental momentum. There are a lot of bass licks, keyboard decoration deep in the mix, odd percussive effects, all of which is perhaps a bit gimmicky but not without charm. Yet try as they might, there's no escaping the lack of a chorus. Sticking instrumental breaks in every third verse isn't the same thing. The original is wonderful, while this is an interesting experiment, an honourable failure.

**'Oh Yeah (On The Radio)'** b/w **'South Downs' (single)**
Personnel: as above
UK and US release date: July 1980
Charts: UK: 5, USA: -
Running time: 4:12/5:14

**'Oh Yeah (On The Radio)'** (Ferry)
A renamed (note the parenthesis) and lightly edited version of the album cut, with the excisions making little difference to the overall effect. This is the version that appears on all later Roxy/Ferry compilations.

**'South Downs'** (Ferry)
A negligible synth instrumental that has been trotted out on several different Roxy and Ferry B-sides over the years.

**'The Same Old Scene'** b/w **'Lover' (single)**
Personnel: as above
UK release date: November 1980
US release date: not released
Charts: UK: 12, USA: -
Running time: 4:00/4:29

**'The Same Old Scene'** (Ferry)
Except for the addition of 'The' to the title, this is identical to the album version. This single was not released in the US, which instead got the album version of 'In the Midnight Hour' backed by 'Flesh And Blood'. In light of that fact, it was odd to find it replacing 'Virginia Plain' for the North American dates of Roxy's $50^{th}$-anniversary tour.

**'Lover'** (Ferry, Manzanera)
A snappy and largely instrumental throwaway, with a drum machine and ringing guitars talking to one another out of sharply separated channels. Mackay's sax in the middle section is a nice mirroring of the main melody. The lyrics are generic hold-me-close-tonight mediocrity – part of the sonic wallpaper more than a song. But it's also much better than half the tracks on the parent album, which makes it a first for a Roxy B-side.

**'Jealous Guy'** b/w **'To Turn You On' (single)**
Personnel:
Bryan Ferry: voice, keyboards
Phil Manzanera: guitar
Andy Mackay: saxophone
Gary Tibbs: bass
Andy Newmark: drums
Produced by Roxy Music
UK and US release date: February 1981
Charts: UK: 1, USA: 80
Running time: 6:10/4:14
John Lennon's murder on 8 December 1980 stunned the world. I still remember teachers weeping inconsolably at the news. It was my first glimpse of the power popular music could have in grown-ups' lives. Roxy's response to the tragedy was to record this cover version of Lennon's 'Jealous Guy', which they had introduced to the live set in December 1980 during German dates in support of *Flesh + Blood*. They went into the studio to record their live arrangement early in 1981, releasing it in February with the *Flesh + Blood* offcut 'To Turn You On' on the B-side. 'Jealous Guy' was immediately embraced by a public still deep in mourning for the slain Beatle, and it became Roxy's only UK number one, topping the charts for two weeks. Four decades later, Roxy's version is vastly better known than Lennon's original,

which had never been released as a single itself. The song has remained a live staple both for solo Ferry and the reformed Roxy. It was their only release in 1981, and their last until April 1982 when 'More Than This' heralded the arrival of *Avalon* the following month.

**'Jealous Guy'** (Lennon)
It's easy to forget that it's this version of the song, rather than Lennon's original, that is lodged in the popular imagination. First the synth wash, then the electric piano, then a line that Ferry might himself have written: 'I was dreaming of the past'. You know the words, of course – simple, lovelorn, apologetic, but not entirely so. When sung by Lennon, who had, by his own admission, frequently been cruel to women, there's an ambivalence, the possibility that he's making excuses for his own behaviour. Ferry, by contrast, wrings every last ounce of tormented sorrow out of himself and into his vocal, but there's no raised eyebrow to undercut the hamminess: it's indisputably the Ferry of 'My Only Love' rather than 'A Song For Europe'. And yet, and yet… it's still pretty good. Manzanera and Mackay are a big part of why. Yes, the synthesizer is often audibly dominant, but the guitar and sax solos are transcendent. They simply reiterate the main vocal melody, but they do so with such insouciant exuberance that the listener is swept up in the fun.

Finally, there's the famously long playout, with Ferry whistling the melody in minor variations over synth strings. It's meant to be artless and charming, and if you let yourself succumb to that rather than resent the emotional manipulation, it's really rather lovely. What's more, Ferry has always done the whistling routine live – even nowadays, with his voice a mere shadow of its former glory. It would be so easy to mime to a recorded version, and that he refuses to do that is a testament to his seriousness as a performer. One can't really deny that 'Jealous Guy' is a symptom of Ferry's coming blandness, but as symptoms go, it's benign.

**'To Turn You On'** (Ferry)
This song reappeared more than a year later on *Avalon* and was an early example of Ferry's obsessive fiddling with his compositions, sometimes leaving bits of songs or even whole tracks sitting on the shelves for years before dusting them off and giving them a proper release. That phenomenon is particularly obvious on *Avonmore* (2015), which was patched together from material of various older vintages, and is also documented extensively on the deluxe edition of *Mamouna* (2023), which included the *Horoscope* album (abandoned in 1992 after half a decade's labour) and rough drafts of songs that would turn up on *Frantic* (2002) and *Olympia* (2010) as well as *Avonmore*.

This early version of 'To Turn You On' doesn't differ radically from the album version, though it's much more of a pop song, thanks to a more sprightly mix with an emphasis on the higher frequencies and more instrumental separation. The two-bar drum machine intro is missing from this single version, but isn't missed. In fact, its absence makes this version feel much more organic and closer in spirit to the pop of *Manifesto* than the soundscapes of *Avalon*.

## Avalon (1982)

Personnel:
Bryan Ferry: voice, keyboards
Phil Manzanera, Neil Hubbard: guitar
Andy Mackay: oboe, saxophone
Alan Spenner, Neil Jason: bass
Andy Newmark, Rick Marotta: drums
Jimmy Maelen: percussion
Fonzi Thornton, Yanick Étienne: backing vocals
Paul Carrack: piano
Kermit Moore: cello
Produced by Roxy Music
UK and US release date: May 1982
Charts: UK: 1, USA: 53
Running time: 41:56

Though the Roxy story has continued with two major and sporadic minor reunions, this still feels like their actual goodbye. Lucy Helmore, helmeted and with her back to the viewer, gazing into the mist and far away with a falcon on her wrist, was as arresting an image in its way as Kari-Ann Moller had been on *Roxy Music*. As David Hepworth put it recently in his book, *A Fabulous Creation*, 'Such was Bryan Ferry's great achievement. He invented a dream, turned that dream into a cover, and eventually disappeared inside it'. Like *Avalon* – named as it was for the final resting place of King Arthur – that quote makes for a slightly bittersweet epitaph.

Commercially, *Avalon* was a triumph. It was Roxy's second straight UK number-one album and had three successful singles, while slow-but-steady American response took its sales to platinum after a decade. Artistically, it's the apotheosis of Roxy Mk III – everything Ferry had been hearing in his head when the band got back together in 1979 brought to life in the studio. For the 40 years since, Ferry has been chasing *Avalon*'s synthesis of sound, space and barely-there vocals with every release, but he's never quite caught it again. That *Avalon* is perfect is beyond dispute. One must, of course, put aside any expectation of a return to *For Your Pleasure* or even *Siren*. This is not an album of ideas or even of songs; it's an album of sound. The studio was the main instrument. That much should've been clear just from the recording venues. It wasn't Manzanera's rough-and-ready Gallery in London, but the Power Station in New York and Compass Point in Nassau – which is to say, two of the world's most expensive and luxuriously-appointed studios.

Over the following decade and beyond, Ferry's search for perfection became paralysing, with him stitching bits and pieces of sound together from hundreds of hours of recordings laid down by the cream of the music business. There are definitely premonitions of that here, on both the proper songs ('More Than This', 'Avalon', 'Take A Chance With Me') and the mood-

and-groove pieces ('The Space Between', 'The Main Thing'). Strangely, the two instrumentals ('India' and 'Tara') feel more organic and less bloated with overdubs.

It's rumoured that sessions for the album were tense, with Ferry obsessive and demanding and Mackay and Manzanera increasingly alienated from the process as guest musicians came and went. It's telling that their co-writes are among the more straightforward tracks on the album. The studio wizardry and the wash of sound make this one of the great love albums of all time: the soundtrack to a million romances. What's perhaps more interesting is that for all its aural seductiveness, it's a weirdly unsexual album, the messy physicality of actual sex abstracted from the mix. That paradox was to continue to haunt Ferry's solo albums for years. But what is different about the *Avalon* songs is the way many of them toughened up and gathered shape and focus when arranged for live performance, something very noticeable on the reunion tours.

At the time, no one could have known that this would be Roxy's final studio recording, especially since the tour that accompanied it would be their longest ever and one of their farthest-ranging. The setlist was weighted heavily towards Mk III songs and included one solo track each from Manzanera ('Impossible Guitar') and Ferry ('Can't Let Go'), along with Neil Young's 'Like A Hurricane'. When the tour was over in 1983, with *Avalon* continuing to sell by the truckload, the band dispersed.

A decade and a world away from their debut, *Avalon* remains a delightful, unexpected terminus for Roxy's short but exceptionally fruitful career.

**'More Than This'** (Ferry)
The album's opening track is among its best. There's a chiming guitar figure as the drums and percussion come in, and Ferry strikes up the melody in his now-very-effective falsetto. It's as instantly compelling as any Roxy opener and is one of the few *Avalon* tracks with a fully formed lyric.

I could feel at the time
There was no way of knowing
Fallen leaves in the night
Who can say where they're blowing?

As free as the wind
And hopefully learning
Why the sea on the tide
Has no way of turning

The old winking cleverness is gone, but each couplet of the opening verse works on its own terms. It's wistful rather than mournful, but manages to evoke wind-blown autumn streets and the chill of a winter evening as rain-lashed waves break on the shore. This sense of transience, of not being able to tell where one's going, is mirrored in the second verse:

It was fun for a while
There was no way of knowing
Like a dream in the night
Who can say where we're going?

No care in the world
Maybe I'm learning
Why the sea on the tide
Has no way of turning

And the chorus is sublime: 'More than this/You know there's nothing'. With perfectly judged punctuation from Mackay's sax, Ferry sounds like he believes his own words – that for all the uncertainty and the possibility that love will disappear like leaves in the wind, there is nothing more perfect than the moments in which you feel it. Manzanera's guitar licks over the coda are a limber extrapolation of the opening chord's promise, while the strings and the synth are there to enhance the melody rather than the mood.

The obvious choice for a single, it's also Roxy Mark III's best one.

**'The Space Between'** (Ferry)

This second track is a pure groove number, anchored on Neil Jason's prominent bass riff which dominates throughout, as other instruments pop in and out to service the sound. The lyric is simplicity itself, a hushed refrain that opens the song and then recurs between two identical six-line verses, in which the second couplet is repeated twice:

The way I see it
This relationship ain't right
The space between us
Better close it up tonight

There's likewise a repeated Mackay sax riff that rides the rhythm. Everything else – Manzanera's guitar, Jimmy Maelen's special effects on percussion – is decoration.

**'Avalon'** (Ferry)

Two interrogative guitar notes and a swell of synthesized strings introduce one of Roxy's best-known songs, not least because it has been played at virtually every Roxy and Ferry solo show since this album's release. 'Now the party's over/I'm so tired': one of the great Ferry themes. Between the strings, the percussive embellishments skittering around the bass and drums, and Manzanera and Neil Hubbard dropping in random snippets of tasteful guitar, it feels at times like a yacht-rock blueprint.

As on 'More Than This', the motif of love's transience (real or potential) suffuses the lyric, where the background fades out of focus, the picture changes every moment, and there's no holding the dancing mystery girl who appears out of nowhere.

Rather than sustained solos, Manzanera cooks up a series of highly charged vignettes that introduce the song's various stages. Meanwhile, Mackay sustains a long solo through the whole outro, though it fades in and out of aural prominence in Rhett Davies' spacious mix.

But – and one must be clear on this point – every other element of this stellar track is eclipsed by the late Yanick Étienne's voice. Like so many other Haitians, she had sought a better life in New York City, where she sang and played with various expatriate musicians, only to be chanced upon by Bryan Ferry in the corridors of the Power Station during the *Avalon* sessions. Entranced by her voice, Ferry invited her to sing, and she cut a soaring, full-throated solo over part of the bridge and the entire instrumental playout. It defies description, alas, but once heard, it's never forgotten, and no backing vocalist in Ferry or Roxy touring ensembles (not even Étienne herself at the Hammersmith Apollo on the first Roxy reunion tour) has ever come close to the magic that was bottled in that New York studio. In the same way that Merry Clayton owns The Rolling Stones' 'Gimme Shelter', 'Avalon' belongs to Yanick Étienne. A titanic achievement.

**'India'** (Ferry)

The *Flesh + Blood* B-side 'South Downs' (Ferry's first attempt at composing an instrumental) was trivial – boring rather than bad. In contrast, 'India' is wonderful. Less than two minutes long, it lands perfectly, supplying a requisite pause after the vocal fireworks at the end of 'Avalon'. The distinctive melodic hook is a guitar synthesizer, which Ferry is credited with playing, in harmony with a fretless bass. Dotted around it are actual guitar phrases supplied by Manzanera and Neil Hubbard, while Alan Spenner and Andy Newmark provide an unobtrusive rhythmic foundation. There are a handful of moments for Mackay buried deep in the mix – appropriately so, as the next track (to which 'India' is a sort of introduction) is very much about his saxophone.

**'While My Heart Is Still Beating'** (Ferry, Mackay)

Although Mackay doesn't dominate proceedings on his co-write, almost all of the song's musical impact does indeed come from the way he wraps his sax lines around what would otherwise be an overly schmaltzy arrangement. He's particularly fine on the choruses, where Ferry's languid cry echoes the sax line rather than vice versa.

I'd better have pity
I'd better go easy
I never will lay down
While my heart is still beating

As the lyric sheet reveals, there's not much there, But Ferry's enunciation is so slack that every Canadian I know thinks he's addressing the chorus to a girl named Alberta. Singing as if consonants were too much of a chore to bother with became Ferry's default mode on succeeding solo albums, often with tiresome results. In this setting, and not yet tarnished by over-familiarity, it's actually quite lovely.

The high point of the track – which ends side one of the original album – is Mackay's downbeat solo, where he heads into entirely different sonic territory than on his ringing chorus riff. That same solo is reprised on the outro before he resolves it into a final, cautiously upbeat flourish. As the sax parts could be scaled up and made more forceful, 'While My Heart Is Still Beating' is one of the *Avalon* tracks that fared best in its transfer to a live arrangement.

**'The Main Thing'** (Ferry)

Despite its longevity in both the Roxy and Ferry live sets, 'The Main Thing' is probably the least prepossessing number on the album. Its bass-heavy stomp recalls the weaker moments of the previous two albums. Where the lyrics on *Avalon* generally convey meaning by suggesting mood, and gain resonance thereby, here they're perfunctory: 'Look at my hand/There's a soul on fire'. 'Everybody knows when a good thing's gone/You can really turn me on'. But there's a nice density to the mix, and the percussive decoration is sometimes impressive. Fonzi Thornton's backing vocal is an excellent counterpoint to Ferry. But though Manzanera and Mackay are credited, their contributions are at best anonymous and more often inaudible. Like 'The Space Between', this one is all about the groove, but it's got none of that track's shape and delicacy – it's best heard at high volume on a dance floor or in concert, where you can feel the insistence of the bass, and the rest of it becomes a wash of sound.

**'Take A Chance With Me'** (Ferry, Manzanera)

The third and final single from *Avalon* appears on the album in a much longer version, with a slow-building instrumental introduction that bears a minimal harmonic relationship to the main body of the song. It's a fine composition and one of Ferry and Manzanera's three best co-writes, along with 'Still Falls The Rain' and 'Running Wild'. The circular four-note guitar hook is the kind of nagging earworm that only works when it's good. This one's very good indeed, and you can see how the rest of the track was built around it and the equally arresting arpeggios behind the chorus.

This is also the only track on the album with Mackay on the oboe, and it provides a sinuous and slightly sour commentary on the otherwise upbeat melody, undermining some of the optimism encoded in the interplay of guitar and voice. Ferry's lyric is simple in the right way, and also unusually positive:

In my time, too much love
Has made me sad for so long

I was lost, can't you see?
Through the long lonely night
Heaven knows, I believe
Won't you take a chance on me?

In his customary despairing mode, Ferry would have been expecting the answer to be that no, the object of desire won't take that chance on him. Here, though, he proclaims that all the world 'should learn to love the way I do'. It's Ferry, so of course, the note of doubt remains, but there's a sense of hopefulness as well. It's a five-minute burst of sunshine on a generally drizzly album.

**'To Turn You On'** (Ferry)
And so is this, a song that had been kicking around since the *Flesh + Blood* sessions. First released as the B-side to 'Jealous Guy', it's the one track on *Avalon* that features neither Manzanera nor Mackay, yet it also fits so smoothly into the texture of the album that you don't notice their absence. It might just be because of Rick Marotta's drumming, but there's a vaguely American feel to the music – a reminiscence of the sound Ferry got on *The Bride Stripped Bare*. It's also possible that the references to New York's Fifth Avenue and Broadway – and the use of Fall rather than Autumn to fit the metre – simply predispose a listener to hear the song a certain way. It's a far more verbal song than most *Avalon* numbers, another sign of the earlier period in which it was written. Structured around the 'I'd do anything to turn you on' chorus, Ferry paints some rather nice vignettes:

I could show you in a word
If I wanted to
A window on the world
With a lovely view
From close up inside a single room
With an open book beside
Like you read in school

The 'beside' in the final couplet is a particularly nice touch. He is indeed showing us – not with a word but with several – the picture he's conjured up for us to admire, and for a minute, you realize how little verbal painting there's been on the album so far. Yet there are also ways in which the song fits perfectly with the album's mood: 'I could walk you through the park/ If you're feeling blue/Or whatever'. That 'whatever' is perfect. Does it mean he's willing to do whatever, walk through the park or do something else? Or does it mean they can walk through the park whether his companion is feeling blue or not? That sort of play with antecedents was such a big part of Ferry's early lyricism that one forgets how diligently he worked to banish it and trim back his words to an evocative minimum. Here, he even gets in his old verbal trick of wrong-footing the listener when, in the final chorus, he sings, 'I'd do anything to turn you/Must phone me, you know me', before bringing back the expected 'When things go wrong/I'd do anything to turn you on'.

Rhett Davies took the single mix and tinkered with it enough to make the joins invisible, adding a drum machine track that manages the transition from the previous song and also overlays the ending as it fades into silence.

**'True To Life'** (Ferry)

This is perhaps the strangest track on the album: an odd but weirdly affecting hybrid. It's amazingly wordy – a story song that has never been attempted live, partly because the verses are delivered so quickly that Ferry could never have managed to nail them every time night after night. There's a synthesizer sequence, a forcefully treated guitar chord, and then drums come in, as a Yamaha CP80 electric grand piano plays in unison with Alan Spenner's bass.

The first three skittering verses trip over themselves as Ferry sings about living in darkness in a dancing city of a thousand faces and, of course, about another 'diamond lady' whose name he doesn't know. In a reversal of the album's normal pattern, it's the chorus that slows everything down – a wash of synth and guitars as Fonzi Thornton's falsetto emotes indecipherably in the soundscape, and Ferry sighs 'True to life'. The effect is odd, schizophrenic almost, as if verse and chorus are in different songs, and the echo wrapped around Thornton's backing vocal almost turns it into a sound effect.

There are at least four guitar parts floating around the mix, which gets more thickly layered with instrumentation as Mackay makes a fleeting appearance on sax and Ferry returns on the verse to travel way downtown in search of nothing.

In the final verse, Ferry reveals himself to be a 'poor country boy' telling his story from town to town, a story with a happy ending, or so it emerges:

> Too much luck means too much trouble
> Much time alone
> But arm in arm with my seaside diamond
> I'll soon be home

Ten years earlier, on 'Re-Make/Re-Model', Ferry was trying but could not find his way. These final words on Roxy's final vocal track suggest that he's found it.

**'Tara'** (Ferry, Mackay)
Mackay improvised the beautiful sax solo under which Ferry and Spenner lay down a cushion of synthesizer and gentle bass, and producer Davies evokes the sound of waves lapping on the shore. Perhaps we're supposed to imagine the boat that carries the dead Arthur from Camelot to his final resting place on Avalon. Or perhaps it's meant to evoke the Irish landscape of the sleeve photo, even if its misty loch is a long way from the hill of Tara. Certainly, one recalls the ghostly, fading 'Ta-ra's that echoed over the end of 'For Your Pleasure' a decade before.

Melancholy and ambiguous, 'Tara' is a fitting elegy for a band that had run its course.

### Related Material

**'More Than This'** b/w **'India' (single)**
Personnel: as above
UK release date: March 1982
US release date: April 1982
Charts: UK: 6, USA: 58
Running time: 4:36/1:46

**'More Than This'** (Ferry)
This is a somewhat different mix of the album version, with a notably different guitar sound and a chorus guitar effect over the outro, which also lasts a few seconds longer. The Pre-Raphaelite picture sleeve reproduces Dante Gabriel Rossetti's *Veronica Veronese*, with Alexa Wilding swathed in a bottle-green dress, idly plucking a violin while looking out of frame, meditative and perhaps disconsolate. As with Roxy's best sleeve art, it adds a touch of new meaning to the music within.

**'India'** (Ferry)
This is identical to the studio version. The US release of 'More Than This' had no picture sleeve and substituted 'Always Unknowing' on the B-side.

**'Avalon'** b/w **'Always Unknowing' (single)**
Personnel: as above
UK release date: June 1982
US release date: not released
Charts: UK: 12, USA: -
Running time: 4:16/5:21

**'Avalon'** (Ferry)
Another slightly different mix from the album version, Ferry's vocal is further forward in the soundstage. On the instrumental middle section, there is an additional track of Yanick Étienne's backing vocals.

**'Always Unknowing'**
A brooding, largely instrumental meander of a track, this sounds like a demo rather than a fully worked-out composition. Ferry's lyric ('Following the morning star/But there's no sense in always running) is the kind of half-written thing that might be alright for a guide vocal. A song it does not make.

**'Take A Chance With Me'** b/w **'The Main Thing' (single)**
Personnel: as above
UK and US release date: September 1982
Charts: UK: 26, USA: 104
Running time: 3:43/3:54

**'Take A Chance With Me'** (Ferry/Manzanera)
This was an almost indistinguishable remix, with no additional instrumentation and with almost a minute of intro and outro edited out, making for a much punchier song. The US single edit (2:46) was even more brutally abridged and less effective as a result.

**'The Main Thing'** (Ferry)
Yet another remix of an album track, this does little to change the somewhat stodgy funk of the original. In the US, the album version of 'India' served as the B-side.

# Conclusion

Roxy toured *Avalon* relentlessly between August 1982 and May 1983, taking in much of western Europe, an abbreviated British jaunt, seven Japanese dates, and their most comprehensive North American tour ever, including almost all of Canada's major cities. And then they stopped. This being Roxy Music, there was no breakup, no mudslinging in the press, no particular drama.

Ferry disappeared into family life with Lucy Helmore and their growing brood of sons, emerging only for a brief and underwhelming performance at Live Aid. In 1985, *Boys And Girls* was a commercial success in most markets, its first single, 'Slave To Love', becoming a radio and film soundtrack staple. He next toured in support of *Bête Noire* (1987) and has gone on the road fairly reliably every two years or so ever since.

After *Avalon*, Manzanera and Mackay continued to play together sporadically as The Explorers and Manzanera/Mackay. Mackay – who had published an innovative book, *Electronic Music: The Instruments, The Music, And The Musicians*, in 1981 – then went on to complete a degree in divinity, while Manzanera became an increasingly sought-after producer. In 2012, a track from his 1978 album *K-Scope* was sampled for the Jay-Z/Kanye West collaboration 'No Church In The Wild', suddenly earning Manzanera more money than three decades of Roxy Music had ever done.

In the meantime, a steady crop of reissues, live albums and compilations has kept the Roxy brand in the shops with varying degrees of success, whether artistic or commercial. A brief overview of archive and live releases would have to start with *Greatest Hits* (1977), which remains the best short introduction to Roxy Mks I and II. Though it was never released on CD, second-hand vinyl copies are inexpensive and widely available, and the track list is peerless and very thoughtfully sequenced: 'Virginia Plain', 'Do The Strand', 'All I Want Is You', 'Out Of The Blue', a remix of 'Pyjamarama' and 'Editions Of You' on the first side, and 'Love Is The Drug', 'Mother Of Pearl', 'A Song For Europe', an edit of 'The Thrill Of It All' and 'Street Life' on the second. *The Atlantic Years* (1983) was released in the US and Canada in an attempt to consolidate Roxy's North American status post-*Avalon*. It adds 'Do The Strand' and 'Love Is The Drug' to four tracks from *Manifesto* and four from *Flesh + Blood*, but not the best four in either case.

In March 1983 – a few months before the *Avalon* tour ended and Roxy ceased to exist – they released the live mini-LP *The High Road*, recorded at the Glasgow Apollo the previous September. It's an odd curio, featuring their cover of Neil Young's 'Like A Hurricane', a long and tedious 'My Only Love', 'Can't Let Go' from Ferry's solo album *The Bride Stripped Bare*, and a very fine rendition of 'Jealous Guy'. Seven years later, *Heart Still Beating* (1990) was a full album of *Avalon* tour material, purportedly recorded in Fréjus in France, but rumoured to have been stitched together from several European dates. That might be true, as the version of 'Like A Hurricane' sounds suspiciously close to the one from Glasgow on *The High Road*. A

CD single of 'Love Is The Drug' taken from the album included an otherwise unreleased live take of 'Do The Strand' from the same tour. Taken individually or together, these releases (and several bootlegs of other tour dates) confirm what Allan Jones said in a scathing *Melody Maker* review about the Fréjus concert that was eventually released as *Heart Still Beating*: *Avalon* 'is recreated in concert as a glossy charade, the group's formerly flamboyant kinetic energy replaced by a dour professionalism'. Jones was right. In contrast with the performances on *Viva!* (which can be compared directly on 'Both Ends Burning', which appears on both albums), the 1982 shows are dull and stuffed with showbiz glitz – the band is too large, the arrangements are overblown, and Ferry sounds bored. Worth hearing as documents of their moment, there's not much pleasure to be had in repeated exposure to them.

After that, the compilations kept coming. *Street Life: 20 Greatest Hits* (1986) was released to capitalise on the success of Ferry's 'Slave To Love' single and its parent album *Boys And Girls* (1985). Combining Roxy tracks with Ferry solo numbers, it progresses more-or-less chronologically, and while the song choice is flawless, and the edits to several tracks are inoffensive, the overall effect is choppy and uneven: 'Street Life' sits oddly next to 'Let's Stick Together' and 'Smoke Gets In Your Eyes', to take just one example of the unhelpful sequencing.

*Street Life* sold very well and so a follow-up, *The Ultimate Collection* (1988), was released to mark the end of Ferry's relationship with E.G. Management and their E.G. label. Like *Street Life*, this collection mixed solo and Roxy efforts, including lesser-known solo singles like 'Tokyo Joe' and 'Help Me', *The Bride Stripped Bare* outtake 'He'll Have To Go', and a very 1980s style remix of 'Let's Stick Together'. There is no obvious logic to the non-chronological running order, which means it coheres less well than *Street Life*. Along with *The Atlantic Years,* it's the only Roxy/Ferry compilation with nothing at all to recommend it.

*More Than This* (1995) was yet another similar compilation, duplicating much of what was already on *Street Life*, this time to promote Ferry's solo releases *Taxi* (1993) and *Mamouna* (1994).

In the mid-1990s, as the repackaging of rock history for the era of the compact disc was reaching its peak, the industry accelerated its output of retrospective, multi-disc compilations, a format that had been pioneered by the Bob Dylan *Biograph* set in 1985. Once the supply of platinum-selling artists was exhausted, it was the turn of the commercial middle tier, Roxy included. *The Thrill Of It All* (1995) was a four-disc set bound as a hardcover book, which included a track-by-track commentary by Ferry. The first disc is the *Roxy Music* album minus 'The Bob (Medley)', 'Would You Believe?', and 'Bitter's End' and *For Your Pleasure* minus 'Grey Lagoons'. The second disc is Roxy Mk II – which is to say *Stranded* minus 'Psalm' and 'Serenade', *Country Life* minus 'If It Takes All Night' and 'Triptych', plus five odd selections from *Siren*. Disc three is Roxy Mk III, with six tracks from each of the three late-period albums. At the time, disc four was the real treat for fans, featuring single

A- and B-sides, almost none of which had appeared on CD previously. The whole set was remastered by Bob Ludwig, who was to also oversee the remastering of the band's album catalogue in 1999. Good though it was to have the rarer tracks in the new format, the set still seemed like a lost opportunity, since adding a fifth disc would have allowed for the inclusion of everything the band ever recorded and also preserved more of the scope and structure of the original albums.

The Bob Ludwig remasters of the eight original albums that came out on CD in 1999 generally avoid the excessive sonic compression that plagued remasters in the late 1990s and early 2000s. There is no obvious distortion or loss of sonic detail in the Ludwig versions, although they are certainly mastered more loudly than the original 1980s CD issues, which always sounded surprisingly good for products of the very early compact disc era.

Ludwig's remastered tracks were also used on the budget compilation *The Early Years* (2000), which is actually rather a good distillation of the first three albums. It includes the five relatively accessible tracks from *Roxy Music*, the singles 'Virginia Plain' and 'Pyjamarama', the best of *For Your Pleasure* (with, however, a full, unedited 'The Bogus Man'), and the three songs one would expect from *Stranded* ('Street Life', 'A Song For Europe', and 'Mother Of Pearl'). And it ends, delightfully, with that album's little-heard 'Sunset'. Although the material is entirely familiar to Roxy fans, the collection is highly recommended to anyone who needs an introduction to what made the early incarnations of the band so special.

At the end of the 1990s, a variety of overlapping and largely redundant live releases appeared, documenting Roxy's *Musikladen* appearances of 1972-1974 and the North American leg of the *Manifesto* tour. These were legal but unsanctioned by the band, so-called 'grey area' releases rather than out-and-out bootlegs. Of the various *Musikladen* collections (*Psalm*, *Vintage*, *Valentine* and *Reflection*), *Reflection* is the most complete. The *Manifesto* concerts (*Alive In America*, *Concert Classics*, *Concerto*, *Ladytron*, *Live In America*, *Live In Denver* and *Showing Out*) are best heard on the double-CD *Concerto* (2001), which is the most complete version of their Denver show from that tour. The sound is FM radio broadcast quality, without much bottom end, but entirely acceptable. It's worth hearing for the way the band re-make/re-model Roxy Mk I and II tracks into funky, Roxy Mark III versions. The interaction of Paul Thompson on drums with touring bassist Gary Tibbs (he appeared on only one Roxy studio recording) is fascinating, especially on the extended instrumental workouts that conclude 'Out Of The Blue' and 'Ladytron'. In terms of arrangements, the segue from 'Stronger Through The Years' into the opening oboe solo of 'Ladytron' is especially good. If nothing else, *Concerto* demonstrates how much inventiveness and personality were lost between the *Manifesto* and the *Avalon* tours, and it makes for much better repeated listening than does *Heart Still Beating*. That said, none of the foregoing releases is essential by any means.

Then, in 2001, the big news arrived – Roxy were to reunite for a lavish tour, which turned out to be extremely successful. As a teaser for the tour and a preview of the potential setlist, the band put out an 18-track *Best Of* in June 2001, including every UK single A-side (except for 'Trash' and 'Take A Chance With Me'), and adding the album tracks 'Out Of The Blue', 'Mother Of Pearl', 'Do The Strand' and 'Re-Make/Re-Model'. Oddly, the songs appear in reverse chronological order, which is thoroughly disconcerting, though the remastering helps smooth over the very different dynamics of the original recordings. The set was issued on vinyl for the first time in 2022 as a double LP with a half-speed master.

Two years after the tour, in 2003, a double-CD souvenir of the reunion tour was released as *Roxy Music Live*. It contains all 22 songs from which the setlists were drawn. Recorded at multiple shows, it was sequenced and mastered as if it were a single continuous concert, and it sounds magnificent. In his late fifties at the time, Ferry remained in robust voice, as he would shortly prove on *Frantic* (2002), his best solo album since the 1970s. Mackay had found his interest in the Roxy legacy rekindled by his role on the soundtrack for the fictionalized glam rock movie *Velvet Goldmine* (1998), while Manzanera, who with his highly successful production career to sustain him had always professed himself open to reunions, here played magnificently. The return of Paul Thompson, meanwhile, noticeably improved the *Flesh + Blood* and *Avalon* tracks, especially 'Oh Yeah' and 'Avalon' itself. The supporting players are also uniformly excellent, especially Lucy Wilkins on violin and keyboards, Julia Thornton on percussion and keyboards, and the ever-reliable Chris Spedding on rhythm (and occasional lead) guitar. A chorus of four backup singers, including the great Yanick Étienne, provides a rich and rounded fullness to the sound. Along with virtually all the songs included on the previous year's *Best Of*, the album adds fantastic versions of 'In Every Dream Home A Heartache' and 'If There Is Something' and an unexpected 'For Your Pleasure' to close. The standout, though, is a sublime rendition of 'A Song For Europe', with a long piano introduction by the tour's musical coordinator Colin Good and an extended saxophone solo from Mackay at the end.

In 2012, the entire Roxy *oeuvre* was re-released as the ten-CD box *Complete Studio Recordings, 1972-1982*. With yet another remaster (a 'flat' remaster, meant to sound as close as possible to the original vinyl releases), this compiled all eight studio albums in Japanese-style replica sleeves of the original artwork, along with a two-disc collection of singles, B-sides and alternative mixes. Disappointingly lacking in sleeve notes (it could surely have repurposed a lot of text from *The Thrill Of It All*), it is still an elegant reissue with excellent audio quality.

In 2018, a long-promised deluxe edition of *Roxy Music* appeared – an LP-sized box holding a lavish hardcover book, three CDs and a DVD, with extensive sleeve notes by none other than Richard Williams, author of Roxy's very first press notice back in 1972. Along with Bob Ludwig's 1999 remaster of the album – which, alas, includes the intrusive 'Virginia Plain' – on the first disc, one bonus disc contains the band's earliest demos from 1971, the ones Ferry had shopped around London unsuccessfully until E.G. Management took an interest, as well as alternative takes of album tracks. A second bonus disc takes in all their BBC recordings from 1972 with somewhat better sound quality than can be found on the several dozen bootleg releases on which they had long circulated. The DVD has all the surviving video of this earliest incarnation of the band, with first Graham Simpson and then Rik Kenton on bass. The only odd omissions are 'The Numberer', the original B-side to the 'Virginia Plain' single, and the unedited, seven-and-a-half-minute version of 'Ladytron', which had been released as a limited edition 10" single for Record Store Day 2015. Their absence means the set falls just short of a definitive document of the original Roxy, though neither one is too much of a loss aesthetically. Fans complained about the cost, but it is a luxurious package, which Ferry supervised with nitpicking attention to detail.

Finally, as Roxy announced their 50th-anniversary tour in 2022, they simultaneously announced a vinyl reissue campaign of all their studio albums. These are prestige affairs, cut at half-speed for the highest audio fidelity, pressed on heavyweight vinyl, and packaged in glossy card-stock sleeves. Every album also includes lyrics on the inner sleeves, four of them for the first time. Vinyl-reissue programs have become the music industry's cash cow of the 2020s, often with shoddy quality control. Perhaps unsurprisingly – given Ferry's perfectionism – the pressing and packaging of these Roxy albums are nearly flawless throughout. *Country Life*, *Siren* and *Manifesto* – which originally suffered from the lightweight and shallow-grooved pressings made necessary by the 1973 oil crisis – are decidedly improved by vinyl of good enough quality to capture their detail.

It remains to be seen whether Roxy will play together again. It seems unlikely, but the response to the 2022 tour was overwhelmingly positive, the performances superb, and the experience seems not to have reopened old wounds. All the original members – even Eno and Ferry – appear to remain on cordial terms with one another, and there's undoubtedly an audience for further shows. With Ferry having published his collected lyrics in 2022 and Manzanera his autobiography in 2024, all concerned seem to be curating their legacies – as well they might, all being in their seventies and with Ferry and Mackay rapidly approaching their 80th birthdays. It would be wonderful if – as they've long promised – they manage to give *For Your Pleasure* the same sort of lavish archival treatment that *Roxy Music* got in 2018. But given Ferry's penchant for micromanagement and procrastination, no one rational would count on it. In contrast, it would be very surprising indeed if a document of the 50th-anniversary shows did not appear, and one can only hope it's put together as sympathetically as *Roxy Music Live* was after the 2001 reunion. In the meantime, pull out a Roxy album at random and have a really good time.

# Bibliography

The following includes every book and article referred to directly in the main text. Johnny Rogan's 1982 book remains surprisingly useful, while the 1976 put-on biography by Ferry publicist Simon Puxley (writing as Rex Balfour) is highly amusing. Simon Reynolds' *Shock And Awe* is one of the best treatments yet of British music in the 1970s. The Buckley, Rigby and Stump volumes each have their uses, though none is consistently accurate, and the Lazell/Rees booklet, while poorly edited, includes many rare photos. Bracewell's book is as much about the intersection of art, music and education in the 1960s and 1970s as it is about Roxy, but it's also scrupulously accurate and very well written. Finally, though an online subscription to *Rock's Back Pages* is expensive, it is well worth it for anyone interested in popular music and the history of music journalism.

Allen, J., 'Roxy Music: 10 Of The Best, (*The Guardian*, 25 February 2015)
Balfour, R. (actually Puxley, S.), *The Bryan Ferry Story* (Michael Dempsey, 1976)
Bracewell, M., *Roxy. The Band That Invented An Era* (Faber & Faber, 2007)
Buckley, D., *The Thrill Of It All. The Story Of Bryan Ferry And Roxy Music* (A Capella Books, 2004)
Cato, P., *Crash Course For The Ravers: A Glam Odyssey* (S. T. Publishing, 1997)
Cavanagh, D., 'The Making Of... Roxy's Music's 'Street Life'' (*Uncut*, November 2009)
Chapman, R., 'Roxy Music. They Came from Planet Bacofoil' (*Mojo*, December 1995.
Chiu, D., 'Running Out Of Steam: Andy Mackay Of Roxy Music On *Siren*', (*The Quietus*, 28 September 2015)
Coon, C., 'Bryan Ferry: Putting On The Style', *Melody Maker*, 12 July 1975
Hebdige, D., *Subculture: The Meaning Of Style* (Methuen, 1979)
Hepworth, D., *A Fabulous Creation. How The LP Changed Our Lives* (Bantam, 2019)
Jones, A., 'Are You Enjoying Yourselves?', November 1982, *Melody Maker*
Jones, A., *Can't Stand Up For Falling Down. Rock 'N' Roll Wars Stories* (Bloomsbury, 2017)
Lazell, B., Rees, D., *Bryan Ferry And Roxy Music* (Proteus, 1982)
MacDonald, I., 'Eno Part I: Before And After Science – Accidents Will Happen', *New Musical Express*, 26 November 1977
Miller, J., *The Rolling Stone Illustrated History Of Rock & Roll* (Random House, 1976)
Moore, A.F., *Rock: The Primary Text* (Open University Press, 1993)
Morrison, S., *Avalon. 33 1/3 no. 155* (Bloomsbury, 2021)
Mulholland, G., *Fear of Music: The 261 Greatest Albums Since Punk and Disco* (Orion, 2006)
Rambali, P., 'Bryan Ferry: The Prisoner', *New Musical Express*, 4 March 1978

Reynolds, S., *Shock And Awe. Glam Rock And Its Legacy, From The Seventies To The Twenty-First Century* (Faber & Faber, 2016)
Rigby, J., *Roxy Music. Both Ends Burning* (Reynolds and Hearn, 2005)
Rogan, J., *Roxy Music. Style With Substance* (Star Books, 1982)
Sinclair, P., 'Andy Mackay and Phil Manzanera in the Roxy Music Interviews' (Super Deluxe Edition, 2018).
Stump, P., *Unknown Pleasures. A Cultural History Of Roxy Music* (Quartet, 1998)
*The Ultimate Music Guide: Roxy Music. From The Makers Of Uncut* (NME Networks, 2022)
Wall, M., 'How Roxy Music Borrowed A Motorcycle And Broke All The Rules', *Classic Rock* (September, 2023)

Also available from Sonicbond

## On Track Series

Allman Brothers Band – Andrew Wild 978-1-78952-252-5
Tori Amos – Lisa Torem 978-1-78952-142-9
Aphex Twin – Beau Waddell 978-1-78952-267-9
Asia – Peter Braidis 978-1-78952-099-6
Badfinger – Robert Day-Webb 978-1-878952-176-4
Barclay James Harvest – Keith And Monica Domone 978-1-78952-067-5
Beck – Arthur Lizie 978-1-78952-258-7
The Beatles – Andrew Wild 978-1-78952-009-5
The Beatles Solo 1969-1980 – Andrew Wild 978-1-78952-030-9
Blue Oyster Cult – Jacob Holm-Lupo 978-1-78952-007-1
Blur – Matt Bishop 978-178952-164-1
Marc Bolan And T.rex – Peter Gallagher 978-1-78952-124-5
Kate Bush – Bill Thomas 978-1-78952-097-2
Camel – Hamish Kuzminski 978-1-78952-040-8
Captain Beefheart – Opher Goodwin 978-1-78952-235-8
Caravan – Andy Boot 978-1-78952-127-6
Cardiacs – Eric Benac 978-1-78952-131-3
Nick Cave And The Bad Seeds – Dominic Sanderson 978-1-78952-240-2
Eric Clapton Solo – Andrew Wild 978-1-78952-141-2
The Clash – Nick Assirati 978-1-78952-077-4
Elvis Costello And The Attractions – Georg Purvis 978-1-78952-129-0
Crosby, Stills & Nash – Andrew Wild 978-1-78952-039-2
Creedence Clearwater Revival – Tony Thompson 978-178952-237-2
The Damned – Morgan Brown 978-1-78952-136-8
Deep Purple And Rainbow 1968-79 – Steve Pilkington 978-1-78952-002-6
Dire Straits – Andrew Wild 978-1-78952-044-6
The Doors – Tony Thompson 978-1-78952-137-5
Dream Theater – Jordan Blum 978-1-78952-050-7
Eagles – John Van Der Kiste 978-1-78952-260-0
Earth, Wind And Fire – Bud Wilkins 978-1-78952-272-3
Electric Light Orchestra – Barry Delve 978-1-78952-152-8
Emerson Lake And Palmer – Mike Goode 978-1-78952-000-2
Fairport Convention – Kevan Furbank 978-1-78952-051-4
Peter Gabriel – Graeme Scarfe 978-1-78952-138-2
Genesis – Stuart Macfarlane 978-1-78952-005-7
Gentle Giant – Gary Steel 978-1-78952-058-3
Gong – Kevan Furbank 978-1-78952-082-8
Green Day – William E. Spevack 978-1-78952-261-7
Hall And Oates – Ian Abrahams 978-1-78952-167-2

Hawkwind – Duncan Harris 978-1-78952-052-1
Peter Hammill – Richard Rees Jones 978-1-78952-163-4
Roy Harper – Opher Goodwin 978-1-78952-130-6
Jimi Hendrix – Emma Stott 978-1-78952-175-7
The Hollies – Andrew Darlington 978-1-78952-159-7
Horslips – Richard James 978-1-78952-263-1
The Human League And The Sheffield Scene –
Andrew Darlington 978-1-78952-186-3
The Incredible String Band – Tim Moon 978-1-78952-107-8
Iron Maiden – Steve Pilkington 978-1-78952-061-3
Joe Jackson – Richard James 978-1-78952-189-4
Jefferson Airplane – Richard Butterworth 978-1-78952-143-6
Jethro Tull – Jordan Blum 978-1-78952-016-3
Elton John In The 1970s – Peter Kearns 978-1-78952-034-7
Billy Joel – Lisa Torem 978-1-78952-183-2
Judas Priest – John Tucker 978-1-78952-018-7
Kansas – Kevin Cummings 978-1-78952-057-6
The Kinks – Martin Hutchinson 978-1-78952-172-6
Korn – Matt Karpe 978-1-78952-153-5
Led Zeppelin – Steve Pilkington 978-1-78952-151-1
Level 42 – Matt Philips 978-1-78952-102-3
Little Feat – Georg Purvis - 978-1-78952-168-9
Aimee Mann – Jez Rowden 978-1-78952-036-1
Joni Mitchell – Peter Kearns 978-1-78952-081-1
The Moody Blues – Geoffrey Feakes 978-1-78952-042-2
Motorhead – Duncan Harris 978-1-78952-173-3
Nektar – Scott Meze – 978-1-78952-257-0
New Order – Dennis Remmer – 978-1-78952-249-5
Nightwish – Simon Mcmurdo – 978-1-78952-270-9
Laura Nyro – Philip Ward 978-1-78952-182-5
Mike Oldfield – Ryan Yard 978-1-78952-060-6
Opeth – Jordan Blum 978-1-78-952-166-5
Pearl Jam – Ben L. Connor 978-1-78952-188-7
Tom Petty – Richard James 978-1-78952-128-3
Pink Floyd – Richard Butterworth 978-1-78952-242-6
The Police – Pete Braidis 978-1-78952-158-0
Porcupine Tree – Nick Holmes 978-1-78952-144-3
Queen – Andrew Wild 978-1-78952-003-3
Radiohead – William Allen 978-1-78952-149-8
Rancid – Paul Matts 989-1-78952-187-0

Renaissance – David Detmer 978-1-78952-062-0
Reo Speedwagon – Jim Romag 978-1-78952-262-4
The Rolling Stones 1963-80 – Steve Pilkington 978-1-78952-017-0
The Smiths And Morrissey – Tommy Gunnarsson 978-1-78952-140-5
Spirit – Rev. Keith A. Gordon – 978-1-78952- 248-8
Stackridge – Alan Draper 978-1-78952-232-7
Status Quo The Frantic Four Years – Richard James 978-1-78952-160-3
Steely Dan – Jez Rowden 978-1-78952-043-9
Steve Hackett – Geoffrey Feakes 978-1-78952-098-9
Tears For Fears – Paul Clark - 978-178952-238-9
Thin Lizzy – Graeme Stroud 978-1-78952-064-4
Tool – Matt Karpe 978-1-78952-234-1
Toto – Jacob Holm-Lupo 978-1-78952-019-4
U2 – Eoghan Lyng 978-1-78952-078-1
Ufo – Richard James 978-1-78952-073-6
Van Der Graaf Generator – Dan Coffey 978-1-78952-031-6
Van Halen – Morgan Brown – 9781-78952-256-3
The Who – Geoffrey Feakes 978-1-78952-076-7
Roy Wood And The Move – James R Turner 978-1-78952-008-8
Yes – Stephen Lambe 978-1-78952-001-9
Frank Zappa 1966 To 1979 – Eric Benac 978-1-78952-033-0
Warren Zevon – Peter Gallagher 978-1-78952-170-2
10cc – Peter Kearns 978-1-78952-054-5

**Decades Series**
The Bee Gees In The 1960s – Andrew Mon Hughes Et Al 978-1-78952-148-1
The Bee Gees In The 1970s – Andrew Mon Hughes Et Al 978-1-78952-179-5
Black Sabbath In The 1970s – Chris Sutton 978-1-78952-171-9
Britpop – Peter Richard Adams And Matt Pooler 978-1-78952-169-6
Phil Collins In The 1980s – Andrew Wild 978-1-78952-185-6
Alice Cooper In The 1970s – Chris Sutton 978-1-78952-104-7
Alice Cooper In The 1980s – Chris Sutton 978-1-78952-259-4
Curved Air In The 1970s – Laura Shenton 978-1-78952-069-9
Donovan In The 1960s – Jeff Fitzgerald 978-1-78952-233-4
Bob Dylan In The 1980s – Don Klees 978-1-78952-157-3
Brian Eno In The 1970s – Gary Parsons 978-1-78952-239-6
Faith No More In The 1990s – Matt Karpe 978-1-78952-250-1
Fleetwood Mac In The 1970s – Andrew Wild 978-1-78952-105-4
Fleetwood Mac In The 1980s – Don Klees 978-178952-254-9
Focus In The 1970s – Stephen Lambe 978-1-78952-079-8

Free And Bad Company In The 1970s – John Van Der Kiste 978-1-78952-178-8
Genesis In The 1970s – Bill Thomas 978178952-146-7
George Harrison In The 1970s – Eoghan Lyng 978-1-78952-174-0
Kiss In The 1970s – Peter Gallagher 978-1-78952-246-4
Manfred Mann's Earth Band In The 1970s – John Van Der Kiste 978178952-243-3
Marillion In The 1980s – Nathaniel Webb 978-1-78952-065-1
Van Morrison In The 1970s – Peter Childs - 978-1-78952-241-9
Mott The Hoople And Ian Hunter In The 1970s –
John Van Der Kiste 978-1-78-952-162-7
Pink Floyd In The 1970s – Georg Purvis 978-1-78952-072-9
Suzi Quatro In The 1970s – Darren Johnson 978-1-78952-236-5
Queen In The 1970s – James Griffiths 978-1-78952-265-5
Roxy Music In The 1970s – Dave Thompson 978-1-78952-180-1
Slade In The 1970s – Darren Johnson 978-1-78952-268-6
Status Quo In The 1980s – Greg Harper 978-1-78952-244-0
Tangerine Dream In The 1970s – Stephen Palmer 978-1-78952-161-0
The Sweet In The 1970s – Darren Johnson 978-1-78952-139-9
Uriah Heep In The 1970s – Steve Pilkington 978-1-78952-103-0
Van Der Graaf Generator In The 1970s – Steve Pilkington 978-1-78952-245-7
Rick Wakeman In The 1970s – Geoffrey Feakes 978-1-78952-264-8
Yes In The 1980s – Stephen Lambe With David Watkinson 978-1-78952-125-2

## On Screen Series

Carry On… – Stephen Lambe 978-1-78952-004-0
David Cronenberg – Patrick Chapman 978-1-78952-071-2
Doctor Who: The David Tennant Years – Jamie Hailstone 978-1-78952-066-8
James Bond – Andrew Wild 978-1-78952-010-1
Monty Python – Steve Pilkington 978-1-78952-047-7
Seinfeld Seasons 1 To 5 – Stephen Lambe 978-1-78952-012-5

## Other Books

1967: A Year In Psychedelic Rock 978-1-78952-155-9
1970: A Year In Rock – John Van Der Kiste 978-1-78952-147-4
1973: The Golden Year Of Progressive Rock 978-1-78952-165-8
Babysitting A Band On The Rocks – G.d. Praetorius 978-1-78952-106-1
Eric Clapton Sessions – Andrew Wild 978-1-78952-177-1
Derek Taylor: For Your Radioactive Children –
Andrew Darlington 978-1-78952-038-5

The Golden Road: The Recording History Of The Grateful Dead – John Kilbride 978-1-78952-156-6

Iggy And The Stooges On Stage 1967-1974 – Per Nilsen 978-1-78952-101-6

Jon Anderson And The Warriors – The Road To Yes – David Watkinson 978-1-78952-059-0

Magic: The David Paton Story – David Paton 978-1-78952-266-2

Misty: The Music Of Johnny Mathis – Jakob Baekgaard 978-1-78952-247-1

Nu Metal: A Definitive Guide – Matt Karpe 978-1-78952-063-7

Tommy Bolin: In And Out Of Deep Purple – Laura Shenton 978-1-78952-070-5

Maximum Darkness – Deke Leonard 978-1-78952-048-4

The Twang Dynasty – Deke Leonard 978-1-78952-049-1

*And Many More To Come!*

## Would you like to write for Sonicbond Publishing?

At Sonicbond Publishing we are always on the look-out for authors, particularly for our two main series:

On Track. Mixing fact with in depth analysis, the On Track series examines the work of a particular musical artist or group. All genres are considered from easy listening and jazz to 60s soul to 90s pop, via rock and metal.

On Screen. This series looks at the world of film and television. Subjects considered include directors, actors and writers, as well as entire television and film series. As with the On Track series, we balance fact with analysis.

While professional writing experience would, of course, be an advantage the most important qualification is to have real enthusiasm and knowledge of your subject. First-time authors are welcomed, but the ability to write well in English is essential.

Sonicbond Publishing has distribution throughout Europe and North America, and all books are also published in E-book form. Authors will be paid a royalty based on sales of their book.

Further details are available from www.sonicbondpublishing.co.uk. To contact us, complete the contact form there or email info@sonicbondpublishing.co.uk